1

The Complete
Quality Manual

The Complete Quality Manual

A Blueprint for Producing Your Own Quality System

GERRY McGOLDRICK

FINANCIAL TIMES

PITMAN PUBLISHING

PITMAN PUBLISHING
128 Long Acre, London WC2E 9AN

A Division of Longman Group Limited

First published in Great Britain 1994

British Library Cataloguing in Publication Data
A CIP catalogue record for this book can be obtained from the British Library

ISBN 0 273 60558 5

10 9 8 7 6 5 4 3 2

Typeset by PanTek Arts, Maidstone, Kent
Printed and bound in Great Britain by
Biddles Ltd, Guildford and King's Lynn

It is the Publishers' policy to use paper manufactured from sustainable forests.

To Eit, Marina and Carly,
and all family and friends,
past and present.

CONTENTS

PREFACE

Today's customers expect a high level of quality whatever they are buying. No longer is it acceptable to deliver 'some time next week'; we are now expected to deliver what the customer wants when the customer wants it. These demands for better quality affect all companies requiring changes in attitudes and organisation. Many have been able to make the necessary changes but, for others, it has been a case of 'too little too late'.

Some have 'blamed' the Japanese for this pressure to improve quality. After all, their ability to produce 'quality' products has decimated many companies and has left us all with something eastern in our homes. Most people, however, think otherwise and have had the sense to learn from the far Eastern countries, particularly their management of quality.

The basis of far Eastern quality has been to deliver reliable products that serve their purpose – a television that always works or a car that always starts. Their methods are not amazingly ingenious, but simply revolve around getting it right first time. Although many far Eastern methods relate to their culture, their objective – getting it right first time – can be universally achieved.

In the Western world, we have finally woken up to what quality really is. Through our own developed management knowledge and learning from the eastern competition, guidelines have been established on how to improve quality. These guidelines, available from the International Standards Organisation, can be used by businesses to achieve the quality goal.

The focus of this book is to explain these guidelines and to aid you, the reader, to introduce a framework to manage quality. The following introduction explains how to define quality and a way of implementing it in your company. The main text of the book concerns writing a reference manual that you can use to manage quality.

Technical terms are avoided where possible, but are explained when they are used. Numerous examples relating to a fictitious company illustrate the text and clarify the subject of quality. After reading the book, you will not only understand quality, but you will also be able to improve your business.

INTRODUCTION

WHAT IS QUALITY?

Of all the business buzz-words, quality is probably the most used (and abused). We hear of 'quality' companies, 'quality' cars etc., but usually nobody mentions what they mean by 'quality'. In this book we use 'quality' to mean being 'fit for purpose and safe to use'. *Thus quality, from the supplier's point of view, is the ability always to produce suitable and safe products for customers.* Throughout this book, we place ourselves in the position of the supplier and will establish a system to satisfy our customers, through improved quality.

The customer usually expresses what they want in the form of a purchase order. For the car dealer, this order might state the colour and model of the desired car. The car dealer must also be aware of the conditions implied in the order; that the car is safe to drive, for example. From this simple example, it can be seen that the supplier must be aware of the *expressed* and *implied* conditions of the customer's order.

The two definitions of quality and of customer requirements are at the core of managing quality. Failing to meet either lowers the level of quality and will probably lose customers. Any management system must concentrate on achieving quality through meeting customer requirements.

QUALITY ASSURANCE SYSTEMS

In a typical business there are rules or guidelines used by staff in their everyday work. Usually the company is organised on a departmental basis and the rules vary to suit the departments. The rules provide the methods used to run the business and ensure continuity as members of staff change. Often, some form of business review also exists. This review might be a regular staff meeting, for example, where problems are discussed. Whatever the type of review, it provides an avenue to learn from mistakes and to improve the business. These methods of running and reviewing the business form the basic framework of a company management system.

To manage quality, a similar framework termed a 'quality assurance (QA) system', must be developed. This framework will span all personnel and departments that affect quality. In it, aims and methods to achieve and manage quality are set out. These must be noted in a manual and available to staff if the system is to be successful. Importantly, staff must be trained and obliged to use the system if it is to work. As was stated in the preface, the framework used in this book is operated worldwide. Prior to explaining it in detail, the background of quality management systems is now briefly addressed.

MODELS OF QA SYSTEMS

Over the last few decades many companies have developed 'in-house' models for QA systems. These models were typically developed by large multinational industries, car and military for example, and were designed to ensure that reliable goods could be manufactured in all their worldwide bases. Design of the systems was based on experience and the aim was to reduce the manufacture of faulty goods. (Frequently, they involved heavy use of 'statistics' and hence came the mistaken view that 'quality' revolves around grey-haired engineers.)

The central principle of these QA systems is that quality cannot be 'tested' into a product (by simply discarding any faulty items). Instead, quality must be 'designed' into the business.

Designing quality means adapting all the parts of the business to supply quality goods and services consistently. Each department, such as purchasing for example, must be addressed and procedures introduced to manage its quality level. Referring to the original definition of quality – providing products fit for use – this means it must be ensured that the purchasing department only orders the correct raw materials.

The older QA systems had much in common and in recent years countries, rather than just companies, decided to form their own models. These drew heavily on local trends and were published as local codes of practice or standards. Each country then encouraged their local businesses to use these models when establishing QA systems. This was a major move forward in recognising the importance of quality management systems. The one remaining disadvantage was that, as a customer, you could not be guaranteed that the 'quality', as defined in one country, always matched that of another.

Finally, and more recently, many countries worldwide have adopted similar or, often, identical international standard models of QA systems. This major step has greatly increased the possibility of increased cross-border trade and, as a bonus, has put pressure on everyone to improve quality. Most large companies now insist that suppliers have QA systems and it is only a matter of time before it will become a prerequisite for everyone to trade. This 'international' system forms the basis of this book and is now addressed.

ISO9000 AND BS5750

The British Standards Institution (BSI), based in the UK, have been the driving force behind this international system. They originally designed a group of standards termed the 'BS5750' series. The main sections of these standards are Parts 1, 2 and 3, based on the functions carried out in three different categories of business. These three standards describe the business functions that must be addressed in a Quality Management system in order to achieve a reasonable level of quality. They are applicable across the full business spectrum and acknowledge that different types of business contain different functions.

The International Standards Organisation (ISO) is an organisation involved in publishing standards or codes of practice for use worldwide. One of its aims is to encourage free trade by the use of such standards. Over the last decade it has published a number of items relating to quality assurance. The ISO have adopted BS5750 Parts 1, 2 and 3, and published them under the ISO9000 series (ISO9001/2/3). In Europe the BS5750 series has also been published as Euronorms in the EN29000 (EN29001/2/3) series. As each set of standards are accepted as reflecting the same level of quality, they are addressed under the ISO9000 banner in this book. Any reference to the ISO9000 standards in this book thus also refers to its BS5750 and EN29000 equivalent.

The application of each ISO standard is based on the primary functions carried out in three different categories of business, as shown in

Standard reference and title	Example industries
ISO9001 Quality systems – model for quality assurance in design/development, production, installation and servicing	Design and manufacturing and/or installation; realty, service (design, marketing etc.) industries
ISO9002 Quality systems – model for quality assurance in production and installation	Manufacturing only or manufacturing and installation only
ISO9003 Quality systems – model for quality assurance in final inspection and test	Warehousing and distribution, installation only companies

Figure 1 Typical industry applications of ISO standards

Figure 1. It is up to you to decide which is relevant to your company – all three are regarded as being of equal status. In most cases, the choice is obvious; if unable to select a standard, look at your competitors and match their standard or seek external advice.

Although the standards are accepted worldwide, some countries, for reasons best known to their government bureaucrats, still use 'local' references as well as the ISO reference. However, the ISO9000 and BS5750 standards are now recognised and used in most of the developed economies, and the reader is advised to use them as the reference standards. Before we analyse the standards in detail, we will now briefly discuss how to promote your level of quality to customers.

COMPANY REGISTRATION

Although the primary purpose of introducing a QA system is to improve quality, you will also want to ensure that your existing and potential customers know that you operate the system. Obviously, you can advertise your system and hope that this will influence your customers. The problem is that although you believe that your QA system is operated correctly, your customers may not! After all, they only have your word that you have met the requirements of the standards. To overcome this problem of credibility, it is advisable to seek 'registration'.

Registration is a formal recognition of your company's QA system and, generally speaking, is a worthwhile exercise. The registration process varies from country to country, but broadly follows the sequence described below.

Initially, the company must write and introduce a QA system to meet the requirements of the relevant ISO standard. The operation of the system must be defined in a guidebook or 'QA manual', as specified in the standards, and staff trained to operate the system. Most businesses will require at least a year to write and introduce the system successfully. As will be seen later in this book, the QA system must be regularly reviewed. During the first year of operation the review helps to iron out the major problems. External advisers are often used during this introductory stage to ensure that the company can comply with the chosen standard. As most of the large management consultancies are now operating in the QA consultancy area, the reader will find little problem in finding a consultant.

When the system is operating successfully, the company must then approach their local registration or assessment body, where they wish to register. The names of these registration bodies are usually available from your local State department for industry and commerce or from your QA consultant. Many management consultancies are also approved as registration bodies. It is best to use these where possible, the benefit being that your consultant will be familiar with the particular registration system in operation.

The next step is a meeting between the company and the registration body. The usual practice is that a questionnaire is completed before or at this meeting. Details of the QA system and the company are queried and discussed at the meeting, including the size and number of sites to be inspected. The cost of inspecting the QA system and the registration fee should be available soon after this meeting. These figures tend to vary a little and it is advisable to get a few quotations.

After agreeing a fee, the company will then be required to submit a copy of the QA manuals and more detailed questionnaires. These are assessed by the registration body for compliance with the chosen standard. Subject to passing this stage, the assessment team will then arrange to visit the company and inspect the QA system in operation. The team is usually made up of at least two trained assessors and, frequently, an 'expert' familiar with the type of industry under inspection. In the company of a member of the management team, elements of the QA system are now inspected. Staff involved in running the QA system will be interviewed in addition to inspecting the use of procedures and customer files.

Note: Inspection of customers' files by external assessment teams may cause legal problems. It is the responsibility of the company to ensure that customer confidentiality is not affected. Any possible problems in this area should be discussed with customers and the assessment team in advance of inspection. In some cases, such as in the medical, legal and accounting areas, written permission may be required from customers prior to introducing your QA system. The electronic and defence industries also tend to be very restrictive, and may even insist on their approval of the assessment team prior to you disclosing any information.

After satisfactory auditing, the company is issued with a 'registered' certificate and is regularly audited by external reviewers thereafter to ensure that the QA system is maintained. The later audits by the assessment team are less detailed and usually occur yearly. Audit fees are about half that of the initial assessment.

Registration is proof from a neutral third party that your system is in operation. It offers credibility and is a sign of your commitment to quality. The registration refers to your method of QA management and does not refer to your ability to produce marketable products. For this reason, it is common practice that you cannot label products with a 'registered' logo. The logo usually appears on letterheads and signage instead. For specific detail on registration in your area, contact your local QA club or chamber of commerce/Department of Trade.

We have now discussed the background of QA and the ISO standards. The standards form the backbone of this book and in the next section – *Using this book* – they are described in greater detail. Hopefully, this introduction will have removed some of the mystery surrounding quality and have encouraged you to use a quality assurance system.

USING THIS BOOK

A FEW TECHNICAL TERMS

Before going further it will be useful to explain the meaning of some common QA terms. Numerous examples, later in the book, will clarify the terms, so don't worry if you are a little baffled initially.

QA system The management information and control system governing all aspects of quality in the business is termed the QA system.

Management representative A senior staff member, termed the 'management representative', must be appointed with the responsibility and authority to manage the QA system. The QA manager usually fulfils this role.

Objectives/policies The main objective is to introduce a QA system to the chosen ISO standard. To succeed, aims or 'objectives and policies' to manage quality in each area of the business, addressed in the standards, must be written down.

QA procedures Objectives are achieved by using written methods. Quality Assurance Procedures (QAPs) are one method used to implement objectives. Typically, QA procedures involve a number of people, as in a design office QA procedure, which might describe the design function.

Work instructions Work instructions (WIs) are another form of QA methods. They usually involve only one or a small group of people, and define methods in the production and installation functions. For example a WI might describe how to weld together steel panels on a car.

QA manual The objectives, policies, methods and associated documents (described later) must be arranged in a reference book. The book, termed a QA manual, acts as the 'bible' for the QA system. As the system develops over time, it must be updated to reflect changes.

For convenience, the QA manual should cross-reference with the ISO standard that the company is implementing.

Controlled documents The QA system will require the use of certain documentation to operate successfully. These include the policies, QAPs, WIs and associated documents. Certain documents, such as the QA manual, are restricted or 'controlled' in distribution.

Contracts Usually customers' orders must be individually identifiable as they are processed from the original purchase order through to dispatch. Whenever a particular customer order in the QA system is referred to, it is called a 'contract'.

Quality audits The complete operation of the business must be inspected, or audited, for compliance with the standards and the manual regularly. Audits are either 'internal'– carried out at the instruction of the QA manager – or 'external' – carried out by the registration body, or customers.

LAYOUT OF BOOK

The book is arranged into four sections, as shown in Figure 2. Most of the book is devoted to explaining a QA system, through addressing each section of the ISO standards and writing the relevant section of a QA manual.

This initial preface and introductory section, which you are now reading, serves as a brief induction to the area of QA and its application. Topics addressed mainly refer to the ISO9000 QA standards and their application in industry. Practical advice on use of software is also discussed, although this is not specifically mentioned in the standards.

The implementation of the QA system is then investigated through each element of the ISO standards. There are numerous examples and the reader should have little difficulty following them. The standards contain many sub-sections, which are often misinterpreted, and to overcome this each sub-section is addressed separately. As an example, when we use the sub-heading 'General' in a module, we are actually addressing a sub-section and not simply making a 'general' comment on QA!

Complete book			
Preface, introduction and using this book	Modules 1 to 20

Description of each element of the ISO9000 standards, with practical examples | QA manual

A 'real' QA manual, with the correct referencing and meeting the requirements of the ISO9000 standards | Index and appendices to the book |

Figure 2 General layout of book

The third section of the book is a 'real' QA manual based on a typical QA system implementation. It is subdivided into three parts, as shown in Figure 3, each containing distinctly separate types of information. This layout is widely used in industry because of its simplicity.

In many cases, the examples used in the previous (modules) part of the book are edited slightly for inclusion in the manual. This is because the examples are simplified to communicate a point. The major difference with the 'real' manuals is that it is correctly cross-referenced.

The final section is the Index and Appendices, which addresses some topics related to ISO9000 QA systems. We now discuss the second section in detail, as it forms the core of learning.

QA manual		
Part 1	Part 2	Appendices
Policy statements for each element of the ISO standards	The methods such as QAPs and WIs used to manage quality and meet our objectives	Samples of forms used in the operation of our QA system. For convenience, these are called 'standard documents' (SDs)

Figure 3 Layout of Section 3 – the QA manual

MODULES

The ISO standards address quality by investigating the different business tasks or 'functions' carried out in a business. A function (e.g. design, purchasing, production etc.) often concerns the work carried

Section in QA standard	QA standard		
	ISO9001	ISO9002	ISO9003
Management responsibility	4.1	4.1	4.1
Quality system	4.2	4.2	4.2
Contract review	4.3	4.3	N/A
Design control	4.4	N/A	N/A
Document control	4.5	4.4	4.3
Purchasing	4.6	4.5	N/A
Purchaser supplied product	4.7	4.6	N/A
Product identification and traceability	4.8	4.7	4.4
Process control	4.9	4.8	N/A
Inspecting and testing	4.10	4.9	4.5
Inspection, measuring and test equipment	4.11	4.10	4.6
Inspection and test status	4.12	4.11	4.7
Control of non-conforming product	4.13	4.12	4.8
Corrective action	4.14	4.13	N/A
Handling, storage, packaging and delivery	4.15	4.14	4.9
Quality records	4.16	4.15	4.10
Internal quality audits	4.17	4.16	N/A
Training	4.18	4.17	4.11
Servicing	4.19	N/A	N/A
Statistical techniques	4.20	4.18	4.12
N/A = Not applicable to this standard			

Figure 4 Comparison of ISO standards by content

out in one department. By adapting and controlling quality in each department, the aim is to manage quality in the business as a whole.

The complete list of functions addressed in the standards is shown in Figure 4. As ISO9001 contains all the functions addressed in ISO9002 and ISO9003, we will concern ourselves with discussing that standard in detail. Referring to ISO9001, we see that there are 20 sections. Each section will be addressed separately in a module in the second part of this book.

Each module describes what is required of your company's QA system to meet the standards. In this book, QA is approached through writing the QA manual. The manual documents your QA system and all the procedures etc. contained in it must be in operation in your company. Modules are introduced in order of appearance in the standards for simplicity. As you will see later, the modules follow a logical path, and we suggest that you introduce your QA system and write the QA manual in the same sequence.

Each module is divided into three main sections as shown in Figure 5. The three sections – function, quality management and summary – take the reader through the topic, assuming that the reader is unfamiliar with QA systems.

The 'function' is a short description of the topic addressed in the module. The 'quality management' area discusses the topic in detail, and introduces keywords and their meanings. (Keywords in italics are of particular importance, as they refer to the ISO9001 standard.) The relevant part of the ISO9001 standard is analysed and hints given on how to introduce this topic into your QA system. This section

Modules 1 to 20:	Function:
Description of each element of ISO9001, including the meaning and use of policies, methods and documents	Brief description of topic under discussion
	Quality management:
	Study of changes in business to implement this topic
	Summary:
	Synopsis of module with hints on implementation

Figure 5 Module contents

includes examples of policies and methods from our QA manual. They are intended only to demonstrate the use of the manual and are simplified for clarity. In practice, many of the examples are combined in single statements and are cross-referenced to other relevant documentation. In addition, the statements would be uniquely identified by issue number and date.

INTRODUCING A QA SYSTEM

The key to quality is an effective management system. This book concentrates on investigating quality through writing the QA manual. As all areas in the business affecting quality are reviewed in the manual, we can learn what is required of each area in a QA system.

From the initial receipt of customer's enquiry through to final dispatch of the finished product, all functions are discussed in detail. To design and introduce your system follow a similar approach. As a first step, try to introduce the concept of quality throughout the business and establish a foundation that can be built on. Then, by successive reviews of each function, increase your awareness and management of quality. Your manual will probably be revised a number of times before it meets the requirements of the standards.

You may require external consultancy advice, particularly when seeking registration. Consultancy can only bear fruit if you have the basics and we would suggest that you at least attempt to introduce quality before using external advice. After all, at the end of the day, *you* have to understand and manage quality, not the consultant.

If you are going to use a consultant, ensure that you control them. In my own experience, consultants have this habit of offering beautiful solutions that can only be implemented over years, and necessarily involve their regular and expensive input. Typically, you should require a consultant for a maximum of 15 to 20 days if you understand the requirements of the ISO standards (hopefully you will, after reading this book). In choosing a consultant, the larger management consultancies do not have any particular advantage over smaller companies. The key is to ensure that the consultant has a reputable background in QA and preferably they should also possess a degree-level or professional qualification. Ideally, they should possess some practical knowledge of your industry, either through other consultancy assignments or business management experience.

USE OF SOFTWARE IN QA SYSTEMS

The use of software tools in all areas of business is now common and, over the last few years, a few companies are producing specialised QA packages. Of the packages available, most appear to have been developed for applications in large, high-technology industries and these are considered impractical in use for most companies. As is the case with much of the business software available, they seem to be able to provide a multitude of reports of little commercial value. Indeed, many include detailed statistics analysis which, as we note later, is rarely required.

The basis of a good QA system is an effective record maintenance and retrieval system. There are a number of simple and relatively cheap database software packages available that are quite suitable for a QA application. These also have the added benefit that they can be used for other applications in the business, thus further reducing costs. Many of our records store valuable data that may also be of use to other business functions such as in marketing, if the data could be easily retrieved. 'Full-text' databases are the best solution if you want to use this data. These software packages permit word-searches across records at lightning speed and are ideal for investigating 'loose' data such as that contained in customer complaint records, where the actual wording of the complaint often hides what you are looking for. If you are going to purchase a package, the advice is to avoid the database software that is expensive to alter in structure. Your requirements will develop over time and there are many relatively cheap database packages available. In operating a QA system, you will also have to design many documents or forms for everyday use (e.g. Customer Complaint Forms). There are a number of software packages available for 'forms design' and many also allow the user to use on-screen forms as an interface to databases.

WRITING THE MANUAL

The manual must be clear and relate to the relevant standard to which you are operating. In this book, the modules are in the order of appearance of the related sections of the standards. Writing your manual to this sequence ensures that it will 'flow' and be organised.

Some modules are easier than others to understand and are treated accordingly. We recommend that you read the book through completely and then decide which section to address initially. As far as possible, make each section of your manual independent of the others; in this way, you will not have too many pages to edit when you come to revise a section.

It is not necessary to have a minimum size to your manual; the only rule is to address all areas in the standards.

MODULE HEADER

The title block of each module contains three separate areas of information. Each is linked to the ISO standards and together they identify the module content, as shown in Figure 6.

The title, 'Design control' (Module 4) in the example, is the formal title of the area of QA systems addressed. Each title has a specific meaning when used in the context of the standards.

The number under the ISO standard reference is the section addressed in that standard. For example, 'Design control' is in Section 4.4 of the ISO9001 standard. If an element under discussion is not required by a standard, the term 'N/A' is inserted. If you are

4 DESIGN CONTROL			
Design planning, input, output, verification and changes	ISO9001	ISO9002	ISO9003
	4.4	N/A	N/A

Figure 6 Typical module header

writing a manual for ISO9002/3, for example, you can ignore the 'Design control' module.

The words in the bottom left-hand box are keywords used in the section of the ISO standard. Thus, in Section 4.4 of the ISO9001 standard, which concerns design control, design planning, input, output etc. are discussed.

USING THE MANUAL

Each document in the QA manual also has a header similar to that in Figure 7. Although the headers differ for each part of the manual, the example shown is relevant to all. The example is derived from actual QA manuals and contains all the necessary data to identify each page of the document uniquely.

The company name 'T. Bear Design & Manufacturing' indicates the 'owner' of the QA system, while the section containing 'Part 2 : QAP # 1' indicates where this document should be placed in the QA manual – Part 2, in the quality assurance procedure section. The title of the QA procedure is then shown underneath.

On the right-hand side, the issue or revision number of the document is shown – Number 2 in the example. The 'Issue date' below this is the date that the document is activated and becomes part of our system. Finally, we also indicate the page number and total number of pages in the document.

In our example manual, we will see that there are many cross-references to WIs and QA procedures. For convenience these are listed at the bottom of each policy statement.

Using a method like this to identify documentation may appear daunting initially, but actually becomes very easy to use once everyone is committed to it. As you will see throughout our investigation

T. BEAR DESIGN & MANUFACTURING	ISSUE #: 2
PART 2: QA PROCEDURE # 1	ISSUE DATE: 1/12/9X
TITLE: REVIEW OF QUALITY MANAGEMENT SYSTEM	PAGE 1 OF 1

Figure 7 Typical title header from the QA manual

of the QA manual and system, it is this commitment that is vital to an effective implementation of QA principles.

You should now have a grasp of quality assurance and its value to your business. The following modules will describe the necessary detail for your QA manual and what is expected of your QA system. We wish you well in introducing quality!

MODULES

1
MANAGEMENT RESPONSIBILITY

Quality policy Management organisation Management review	ISO9001	ISO9002	ISO9003
	4.1	4.1	4.1

FUNCTION

If we wish to introduce any scheme or plan into a company we must, first of all, agree on the rules of the plan and agree to abide by them. The organisation of the business must be defined and a manager appointed to manage quality on behalf of the company. In addition, we must arrange to have a method of monitoring the system.

QUALITY MANAGEMENT

QUALITY POLICY

Our attitudes to quality must be addressed initially. A written statement, signed by a senior manager, stating that we have a quality system and that we follow its rules is required. This is, in effect, a public announcement of the company's commitment to quality. It can be brief but should clearly show our policy towards quality matters. Many companies display it on publicity material and in their front office. A clear statement of only a few lines, as shown in Figure 1.1, will meet the requirements.

ORGANISATION

In every business there is a management structure in operation, even if it is not formally stated. The command structure describing the responsibility and authority of personnel, who carry out work affecting quality, has to be agreed and stated. For the typical business this includes the design, manufacturing and installation functions, as well as the purchasing, financial and sales areas.

T. Bear D & M Company
Management responsibility

QUALITY POLICY STATEMENT

1 It is the policy of T. Bear Design Company to design toy bears at an economic level to standards and design requirements of our customers.

2 In our company we have prepared a quality manual which contains the company's policies and procedures relating to quality.

3 All staff are obliged to adhere to the procedures in the quality manual.

4 Employees and our customers are encouraged to make suggestions that will improve our level of quality.

Signed: J. Bloggs Senior Manager

Figure 1.1 A quality policy statement

Personnel must be assigned responsibility and authority to manage quality through:

1 Preventing the production of low quality produce where possible;
2 noting any problems that occur;
3 providing solutions so that the problems do not recur;
4 checking that solutions work effectively and, finally;
5 regulating output where quality problems have been noted.

These actions can only be carried out by suitably trained staff. The training procedures are addressed in a later module and need only be briefly mentioned in the policy statement.

The command structure is best shown graphically, as in Figure 1.3. Job specifications may be specified in the appendices to the manual. Take care to update these regularly as they change frequently in most businesses.

T. Bear D & M Company
Management responsibility

MANAGEMENT ORGANISATION

1 The company management organisation is shown in Figure 1.3.

2 Job specifications are contained in the appendices to this manual.

3 Staff are assigned responsibility to manage quality throughout the company. Where necessary staff are trained to devise and implement solutions to manage quality.

Figure 1.2 Policy – management organisation

QA MANAGER The company must also have an employee, usually a member of management, who will ensure the QA system is implemented and operated correctly. They have full authority in all QA related matters and answer to senior management.

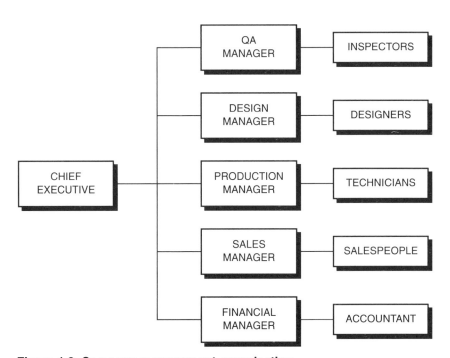

Figure 1.3 Company management organisation

In the QA system organisational structure, this person is known as the 'management representative'. It is good practice to display in the QA Manual the company organisation for quality assurance indicating the managerial position of this management representative. This differs from the previous command structure as it also indicates the lines of communication both internal and external to the company.

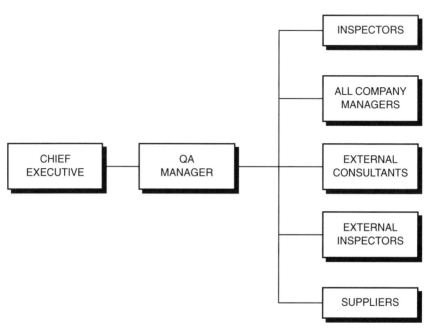

Figure 1.4 QA function organisation

MANAGEMENT REVIEW We now have agreed to a QA system and the organisation used to implement it. Although it might appear obvious, we must also review the operation of the system itself regularly. This ensures that we keep up to date with current industry practice and have a continuous path of improvement. This 'management review', as it is termed, should be clearly stated, as in the example over.

T. Bear D & M Company Management responsibility
MANAGEMENT REVIEW 1　The quality system and its associated procedures and instructions are systematically reviewed at regular intervals to ensure that they are effective and relevant 2　The complete manual, procedures and instructions are reviewed at least once a year. 3　The review records are maintained and controlled by the management representative.

Figure 1.5　A typical management review statement

SUMMARY

The quality policy is a written statement, signed by a senior manager, of the company's belief in quality.

The command structure of the company should be described briefly. In addition, the QA management structure should be shown in a chart with the management representative (QA manager) in a senior position.

The overall QA system must be reviewed on a systematic basis. All reviews should be formally noted.

All of the statements, including the management structures, are 'objectives' and are, therefore, in Part 1 of the manual. Procedures need not be referred to in this module.

The job descriptions can be in the appendices.

2
QUALITY SYSTEM

QA manual, QA plan Instructions, procedures	ISO9001	ISO9002	ISO9003
	4.2	4.2	4.2

FUNCTION

As explained in the introduction, a QA system is simply another type of management information system. Like other systems in a company, it revolves around employees and the methods used by them to operate the system.

Before establishing rules the aims or objectives of the system must first be set. These have already been briefly referred to in the 'quality policy' and are expanded on in this section. We also refer to the quality manual of our QA system, and its purpose, contents, distribution and use. (Note that the individual methods used to control design, manufacturing etc. are addressed in separate modules.)

QUALITY MANAGEMENT

QA MANUAL

The quality system in operation is governed by the contents of the quality manual and documentation referred to within that manual.

The QA system is described in detail, in addition to the operating procedures and organisation structure. By using it as a reference manual you can assess by regular checks whether you are operating to the system rules.

CONTENTS

For convenience, the manual is split into two functional parts.

Part 1 will include the company's policy towards each aspect of the ISO900X Standard. This is the outline guide to the company's activities in pursuing a 'quality' environment. In essence it is the 'bible' of the quality management system.

The specific methods and resources used to carry out the work, referred to as work instructions (WIs) and QA procedures (QAP's) are contained in Part 2. These clearly define the techniques that staff must use in their work. Examples of documents used in the operation of the QA system are also included in Part 2, as well as the appendices to the manual.

ISSUE OF QA MANUAL The methods by which the manual is issued and amended must always be specified. It is normal practice to limit the distribution of the manual to nominated personnel. This safeguards the investment that the company has made in a quality system (including any commercially sensitive information) and provides a regulated list of people to be supplied with amendments to the manual.

The amendment procedures are at the company's discretion, yet should provide the facility to allow controlled but frequent amendment, if necessary.

CONTRACT REQUIREMENTS Finally, mention should be made of 'specific contract requirements'. These are specific conditions in customer orders that require usual QA methods to be adapted. For example, a special quality plan may be required. These quality plans are similar to 'To do' lists. The plan itemises the step-by-step approach required to achieve and control quality for a contract or job element. Figure 2.1 over clearly shows their use.

Where a conflict arises between your system and a customer's order, the method providing the highest level of quality should be used. In these cases, the customer should be notified and an agreement reached, prior to commencing work.

SUMMARY

The QA system is defined in a two-part QA manual. Part 1 contains the QA policies and Part 2 contains methods used to implement these policies.

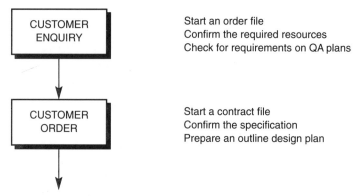

Figure 2.1 Extract of general company quality plan (Apx)

The manual must be issued and amended in a controlled way to ensure all copies are consistent.

A general quality plan will show the normal methods in dealing with a contract. Where additional methods are required by a contract, a specific quality plan can be designed.

A policy statement, as shown in Figure 2.2, is inserted in Part 1 of the manual.

The method to issue/amend the manual should be short and can be described in Part 1. If it is complicated, due to your company structure, it can be described in a QA procedure in Part 2.

The nominated list of those who retain copies of the QA manual usually includes all departmental heads and the QA manager, but as a general rule, it should be available to those who need to consult it regularly. For reasons of confidentiality and control, keep the number of people to a minimum.

The general quality plan should be inserted in the appendices.

T. Bear D & M Company
Quality system

---

1 *The quality assurance manual*

This manual contains the operational methods to run our QA system. It defines the policies and objectives of our company towards quality, and the methods used to realise these. All staff are expected to abide by these methods, except where health and safety rules dictate otherwise.

2 *Manual contents*

This manual is divided into two parts.

Section 1 contains the policies to meet each aspect of quality assurance. As we wish to operate in accordance with ISO9001:1987, all modules are numbered relative to the sections in that standard for convenience.

Section 2 contains all the instructions, procedures and standard documents used within our system.

3 *Issue and amendment*

Distribution is restricted to those in the distribution list on the front page of this manual. The manual is updated on a regular basis. The amendments are distributed by the management representative and must be included in this manual upon receipt.

4 *Specific contract requirements*

The quality plan in Appendix 1 of the QA manual – Part 2 is to be used unless the customer requests otherwise. In all cases the plan achieving the higher level of quality must be used.

Figure 2.2 Quality system statement

3
CONTRACT REVIEW

Investigation of enquiries and orders from customers	ISO9001	ISO9002	ISO9003
	4.3	4.3	N/A

FUNCTION *Contracts are the individual orders received from customers for the goods or services that the company supplies. At the enquiry stage, the tender is checked to see if the company can meet its requirements. These might include delivery dates or specific packaging, for example. As these are translated into contracts, the enquiry must again be matched with the order and cross-checked for any differences. These actions of reviewing the orders are termed 'contract review'.*

QUALITY MANAGEMENT

CONTRACT REVIEW The steps taken in the contract review can be specified in QA procedures. You can refer to these QA procedures and outline your general policy in Part 1 of the manual. Prior to defining procedures, you should contact your present customers, as you may have to arrange your contract review to match their ordering systems. Figure 3.1 shows a simple model policy statement for this module.

The procedures contain the specific actions taken in dealing with enquiries and tenders. Where specific documents such as checklists are used, these should be referenced in the procedure. The examples below relate to customer enquiries, in which a standard form is being used to log the enquiry.

T. Bear D & M Company
Contract review

---

1 All enquiries received are investigated to ensure that sufficient details are supplied to allow us to supply an accurate quotation. Any shortage of data is sought from the source of the enquiry.

2 All enquiries and orders are given a unique reference number. Orders are compared with the related enquiry and any conflicts are clarified with the customer before commencing work on the order.

3 Any contract representing more than 10% of turnover must be reviewed on a weekly basis. All other contracts are reviewed every two weeks.

The relevant QA procedures describing the review procedure in detail are in Part 2 of this manual.

Figure 3.1 Policy: Contract review

T. Bear D & M Company
Customer enquiry procedure

Purpose
To ensure all enquiries are acted upon in a controlled way.

Procedures
All enquiries are logged by the sales manager in a sales enquiry book.

A standard enquiry form, Enquiry Document 1, is completed by the manager noting the relevant details.

The receipt of the enquiry is confirmed in writing.

The enquiry is then passed to the chief estimator.

Figure 3.2 Sample QA procedure #1 re: customer enquiries

```
+-----------------------------------------------------------+
|                  T. Bear D & M Company                    |
|                   Enquiry docuement 1                     |
+-----------------------------------------------------------+
| RECEIVED BY:                      DATE:  /  /              |
|                                                           |
| COMPANY NAME:                                             |
|                                                           |
| ADDRESS:                                                  |
|                                                           |
|                                                           |
| CONTACT:                          PHONE:                  |
|                                                           |
| PRODUCTS REQUIRED:                                        |
|                                                           |
| REPLY BY:  /  /                                           |
+-----------------------------------------------------------+
```

Figure 3.3 Sample standard document referred to in QA procedure #1

SUMMARY

All contracts must be examined prior to commencing any work. The company must be able to satisfy the contract, including all its terms and conditions. Any ambiguities must be clarified with the customer.

Part 1 will contain the policy statement as in the example. This may be short in length, as the relevant procedures are contained in Part 2.

Relevant procedures include those dealing with the methods for processing enquiries and orders. The methods of estimating/pricing may also be included.

4
DESIGN CONTROL

Design planning, input, output, verification and changes	ISO9001	ISO9002	ISO9003
	4.4	N/A	N/A

FUNCTION *Design is the first element of the contract after accepting the customer's order. To control the design process it can be broken down into several individual elements. These are then described and represent your control of the design function. Again QA procedures should detail your specific procedures.*

QUALITY MANAGEMENT

GENERAL Our stated policy is to control all design activities, and ensure that designs meet the customer's requirements and relevant legislation. Any technical libraries or similar sources of information should be organised, up to date and available to the design teams. Specific care should be taken of ISO standards or similar codes of practice to ensure that they are maintained to the issuer's instructions.

PLANNING All contracts identified, by a unique reference, should be planned according to your general quality plan, unless specific plans are requested. All plans should reach the quality level of the general plan. The involvement of staff should be identified with only trained staff or advisers having an input. Each stage of design, from concept to completion, must be addressed, including occasions where liaison with the customer or other companies is required.

| INPUT | The input into the design will include the contract documents and information from the technical

data in your library. Any design decisions agreed at meetings, inside or outside the company, are considered as inputs and must also be noted. In some industries, it is the practice to confirm these design notes in writing to the customer as memoranda. Although this does not place any responsibility to confirm the memoranda, it can vastly reduce the volume of errors and is recommended.

| OUTPUT | Design output includes the drawings, models etc. produced by the design team. These must be

stated as meeting the design brief and any statutory requirements.

| VERIFICATION | Our method of verification of the design must also be stated. This may be done by reference to

previous similar designs and/or by another member of staff double-checking the design work.

| CHANGES | Finally, we must choose a method to control changes in design. The revision of documents is a

very important element of the QA system and must be controlled. A simple method is to affix a 'revision number' to all document reference numbers and increment this at each revision. The revision changes should also be noted, particularly in drawings. Whatever the method, it must show that all input and output documents are clearly identified.

T. Bear D & M Company
Design control

General
The company has adopted procedures to ensure the control of all design activities to ensure we comply with all contract specifications and relevant statutory obligations.

A technical library is available and the company maintains relevant ISO standards for staff use.

Planning
Design jobs are planned according to the general quality plan, unless otherwise stated in the contract. Any other plan must be approved in writing by the management representative.

Input
Designs are based upon the contract specifications and statutory law. In case of conflict, statutory law will prevail and this must be agreed in writing with the client prior to continuing the design.

Output
All design output must comply with statutory regulations.

Verification
The design manager will select the employee who will verify work on a contract. Previous contracts of a similar nature may be used for comparison.

Changes
All design and approval stages must be recorded. Revisions and distribution will be carried out according to our document control procedures

The relevant QA procedure describing the design procedure in detail is in Part 2 of this manual.

Figure 4.1 Policy: design control

T. Bear D & M Company
Design control procedure

Purpose
To ensure that the design function is used to produce designs to customer requirements.

Procedure
The general quality plan is to be used unless the order requires a specific plan.

The design manager will issue a timetable to designers, using the design planning form, specifying the completion dates for the design element of each contract.

Designers must report any delays to the design manager who will then allocate extra resources, if required.

All drawings, models and calculations must be approved by the design manager. Each element must be cross-referenced with the contract.

Where ISO standards or codes of practice are used, these must be referred to in the design output.

The customer's approval must be gained for all drawings, models and calculations prior to passing the design package to the manufacturing department.

Figure 4.2 Design control procedure

T. Bear D & M Company Design planning form		
CONTRACT:	DESIGN COMPLETION DATE	CUSTOMER APPROVAL DATE
DRAWINGS		
CALCULATIONS		
MODELS		
THE ABOVE DATES MUST BE MET TO COMPLY WITH CUSTOMER ORDER		

Figure 4.3 Design planning form

SUMMARY

A general comment on the design control policy is made as an introduction to this module. After that the individual elements of the design process are addressed.

Design planning, input and output are described and documented for contracts. The last stage in a design is the approval stage. This must be carried out with care by trained staff.

Design changes must be identifiable by an unambiguous referencing system that can be easily used and understood by both staff and customers.

The policy statement should only refer to your general policy towards design control. If particular Standards are mentioned in it, this may require frequent revisions of the statement. Each section (inputs, outputs etc.) should be addressed separately.

The associated procedures in Part 2 should refer to the specific planning tools used (planning forms etc.). Where an approval procedure is used, ensure that it meets the requirements of your customers. Approval methods vary from customer to customer and your method should take account of this.

5
DOCUMENT CONTROL

Approval and issue Changes/modifications	ISO9001	ISO9002	ISO9003
	4.5	4.4	4.3

FUNCTION *In any business there are various documents used throughout the duration of a contract, broadly falling into two categories.*

There will be paperwork individual to each contract, such as the customer order or drawings, for example. These are readily identifiable as belonging to the contract.

In the second category, there are documents used with many contracts. These include relevant codes of practice, work instructions and suppliers' catalogues.

In both cases, the issue, use and withdrawal of the documents must be organised. The element of a QA system describing this organisation of documents is termed 'document control'.

QUALITY MANAGEMENT

APPROVAL AND ISSUE All documents should be approved for use prior to being made available to staff. This approval method must be documented (QA procedure). This method not only concerns the document content but must also ensure that documents are issued to the appropriate personnel. The version of each document is termed an 'issue' and all old issues must be promptly removed from circulation as they are replaced. Some documents will have a restricted distribution (e.g. the quality manual) and are termed 'controlled documents'. The procedures must also address these type of documents.

T. Bear D & M Company
Document control

Approval and issue
All documents generated in-house are approved for use by a review
board who will meet at the discretion of the management representative.

The procedures in force ensure that only current approved documents
are used by staff.

All codes of practice and standards are controlled by the drawing office
manager, who is responsible for approving their distribution and use. Only
current standards are to be used unless the contract specifies otherwise.

QA procedures in part 2 address these areas.

Figure 5.1 Policy: document approval and issue

CHANGES AND MODIFICATIONS Often, documents will need to be altered or replaced. These changes must be noted (if possible in the altered document), and the method of review and change must be documented. In addition, the same procedure used to issue the original document should again be used. To ensure that all changes are noted and available to staff, lists of all current documentation must be available.

It is not necessary or practical to make a new issue for each change. Instead, changes should be grouped together and treated as one issue. Staff of the same function (e.g. designers) who originally approved the documents should also carry out the changes/modifications. This will ensure a consistent approach. The examples in Figures 5.2 and 5.3 address each of the above topics.

T. Bear D & M Company
Document control

Changes and modifications
All changes/modifications to documents are reviewed by authorised staff. The staff will, where possible, be those who originally approved the document.

All changes/modifications are recorded as they are made.

Master lists, identifying the current issue, are maintained of all standards and drawings.

The QA procedure in Part 2 of this manual describes the method used to identify changes/modifications in documents.

Figure 5.2 Policy: document changes and modifications

T. Bear D & M Company
Drawing control procedure

Approval and issue of drawings
All drawings must be approved by the design manager, prior to issuing to the customer.

The designer will ensure that drawings are noted in the drawing issue logbook.

A cover note, detailing the drawing title, contract reference and revision number is issued with each drawing. A copy of the cover note is retained in the contract file.

Figure 5.3 Procedure: drawing approval and issue

SUMMARY

Documents must be approved for issue and issued to the staff who require them in their work. Contract documents issued to customers must be treated similarly.

Out-of-date documents must be removed from circulation. As changes/modifications occur they must be noted. These changes should be carried out by the same function that approved the documents.

Master lists should be maintained of current document revisions.

Procedures should be designed to handle different groups of documents. For example, technical literature and standards could be treated separately from drawings and material lists.

It is probable that many forms are used to record the different tasks ('cover notes for drawings', 'drawing issue sheets' etc.). Try to minimise the number of forms when addressing the subject of document control. This not only reduces paperwork, but can also reduce costs. The forms used should be cross-referenced and examples contained in the appendices.

6
PURCHASING

Assessment of sub-contractors, purchasing data and verification of product	ISO9001	ISO9002	ISO9003
	4.6	4.5	N/A

FUNCTION

All goods or services purchased from outside the business must be clearly specified and checked to ensure that they meet requirements. In addition, the suppliers must be reviewed regularly for compliance with your requirements. These functions are addressed in detail in this module, particularly the management of suppliers.

QUALITY MANAGEMENT

GENERAL

A brief comment, as shown, that you operate procedures to control your purchasing function is required. The later sections are detailed and contain all references to procedures.

ASSESSMENT OF SUB-CONTRACTORS

To meet the requirements of QA standards, a formal approach to judging suppliers, termed 'vendor assessment', is needed. This involves assessment of vendors against particular criteria and is now explained in detail.

T. Bear D & M Company
Purchasing

General
The company operates procedures which ensure that all goods and services purchased meet our requirements.

Figure 6.1 Policy: purchasing – general comment

The first step in assessment is to draw up a list of elements affecting the overall service. If we wish, suppliers may be divided into groups, as in the example given in Figure 6.2 for cloth suppliers, and we may use different criteria for each group. For practical purposes, the number of groupings and criteria should be small.

T. Bear D & M Company – Cloth Suppliers Group Service elements for assessment		
Deliveries on time	Range of colours	Range of cloths
Price	Packaging	QA system

Figure 6.2 Cloth suppliers – assessment criteria

Now the criteria are valued or 'weighted' according to their effect on *your* level of quality. The weighting depends on the company's business and can be modified over time. The example has a high value for 'deliveries on time' as T. Bear Co. like to minimise their stock.

T. Bear Co. now have a scheme to 'value' their cloth suppliers and a practical example is shown using a standard form. Your assessments should also be checked for consistency. As the results of assessments

T. Bear D & M Company Assessment of cloth suppliers	Maximum points in total = 100
CRITERIA	WEIGHTING POINTS
Deliveries on time	25
Price	15
Range of colours	10
Packaging	20
Range of cloths	10
QA system	20

Figure 6.3 Weighting of assessment criteria

VENDOR ASSESSMENT REPORT		
T. Bear Design & Manufacturing	VENDOR NO.: 56TGB	
	NAME: CLOTH INC. ADDRESS: 251 MAIN ROAD LONDON	
	DATE: 20/6/9X	

SUPPLIER OF:	WOVEN CLOTH ROLLS AND COVERINGS	

ASSESSMENT FORM G1 ISSUE 1 ISSUE DATE 2/4/9X

ELEMENT	POINTS		COMMENTS
	MAX	TODAY	
DELIVERIES ON TIME	25	15	installing new dispatch system and it is causing some delays
PRICE	15	12	has lowered prices due to devaluation
RANGE OF COLOURS	10	8	extensive range
PACKAGING	20	14	has promised to increase use with the soft cloths
RANGE OF CLOTH	10	8	meets most of our needs
QA SYSTEM	20	15	ISO9001 system
TOTAL	100	72	
GENERAL COMMENTS	he is meeting our requirements and agrees with the criteria used in this assessment.		
SIGNED	J. BLOGGS		

Figure 6.4 Sample vendor assessment form

vary over time it is usual to have a system that reflects change. For example, in the vendor assessment procedure (Figure 6.5), it might be stated that, when a supplier reaches 60 per cent of his maximum points in two consecutive assessments, assessments will be made more frequently.

You must also decide how often to carry out assessments and who will carry them out. Normal practice is to assess suppliers at least yearly. The assessment date should be irregular for accuracy. Where visits to the supplier are required 'surprise calls' can cause problems, unless the supplier agrees to unannounced visits. A happy medium would be to agree with two to three days' advance notice to the supplier of his assessment.

PURCHASING DATA

Although it might be obvious and already practised informally in your business, purchasing data must be clearly specified on orders. The data must be unambiguous and where possible should refer to national or ISO standards. This may be tedious to set up, but can be simplified by drawing up data sheets for the goods/services required. These can then be quoted in the order. Where goods are concerned, ensure that you can identify them to a particular order as they arrive. This might require identification on each item or on their packaging, if bundled. The example in Figure 6.6 is a typical policy statement for this element. The associated procedure would specify the particular method of processing a purchase order in your company.

The examples in Figures 6.7 and 6.8 are of a purchase order and associated data sheet. Note that the specifications are not included in the manual. Instead, it can be stated in the policy statement that they are used. It is advisable, however, to include a sample purchase order in the manual, to be used as a reference.

T. Bear Design & Manufacturing	ASSESSMENT OF CLOTH SUPPLIERS		
	ISSUE: 1	DATE: 23/12/9X	REF NO. 1

PURPOSE	TO ENSURE THAT SUPPLIERS OF CLOTH ARE SELECTED BASED ON THEIR ABILITY TO MEET SPECIFIED REQUIREMENTS AND THAT THEIR PERFORMANCE IS MONITORED	
PROCEDURE	1	THE BUYER MAINTAINS A LIST OF APPROVED SUPPLIERS THAT ARE TO BE ASSESSED ON A 6-MONTHLY BASIS.
	2	ALL SUPPLIERS MUST BE ASSESSED USING THE LATEST REVISION OF THE VENDOR ASSESSMENT FORM G1.
	3	WHERE A VISIT TO THE VENDOR'S PREMISES IS REQUIRED FIVE DAYS' ADVANCE NOTICE IN WRITING MUST BE GIVEN UNLESS OTHERWISE SPECIFIED BY THE BUYER.
	4	SAMPLES OF MATERIAL AND DOCUMENTATION ARE TO BE VIEWED ON ALL OCCASIONS.
	5	WHERE THE TOTAL POINTS RATING IS 70 OR GREATER THE VENDOR REMAINS ON THE APPROVED LIST.
	6	WHERE THE TOTAL POINTS ARE BETWEEN 50 AND 70 THE ASSESSMENT MUST BE CARRIED OUT MONTHLY AND THE VENDOR ADVISED THAT RECURRENCE OF THIS OVER THREE ASSESSMENTS IN ANY ONE YEAR WILL RESULT IN THEM BEING REMOVED FROM THE SUPPLIERS' LIST.
	7	THE VENDOR ASSESSMENT FORM IS TO BE REVIEWED AND MODIFIED WHERE NECESSARY EVERY SIX MONTHS. ALL MODIFICATIONS MUST BE CARRIED OUT USING THE DOCUMENT CONTROL SYSTEM.

Figure 6.5 Sample QA procedure for vendor assessment

T. Bear D & M Company	
DATE: 23/12/9X	PURCHASE ORDER REF: GFSD 324565
PLEASE SUPPLY TO THE FOLLOWING ORDER	
TO: J. BLOGGS BOX MANUFACTURER	
5000 NUMBER PACKING BOXES TO OUR SPECIFICATION XFT 123/ISSUE 1 DELIVERY: 1 WEEK FROM DATE OF ORDER CERTIFICATE OF MEETING OUR STANDARD IS REQUIRED	PRICE AS PER STANDARD CATALOGUE OF 5/5/9X

Figure 6.7 Sample purchase order

T. Bear D & M Company		
SPECIFICATION: XFT 123	ISSUE: 1	ISSUE DATE: 23/12/9X
PACKAGING – SPECIFICATION – BOX SIZES 1 TO 5		
MATERIAL WALL THICKNESS – INDUSTRY SIZE 5		
FIRE RATING: 23A		
LOADING: 40 lb/sq ft or 10 kg/sq m		
STACKING: 20 HIGH TO FIT OUR STANDARD BULK CONTAINERS		

Figure 6.8 Sample ordering specification (example only)

VERIFICATION OF PURCHASED PRODUCT Finally, you need to address the occasions when a customer wishes to examine the goods/services purchased for use in their contracts with you. A simple case in T. Bear Co. would be a customer examining a fabric prior to it being used on their contracts. In these situations, the customer must be given 'reasonable access'. The degree of access will depend on your particular company/industry. As a guide, offer your customers the same degree of access that you demand when carrying out vendor assessments.

Although the customer may 'approve' the materials after examining the goods, it must be emphasised that you are still responsible for the overall quality level. This should be clearly stated as shown in Figure 6.9.

T. Bear D & M Company
Purchasing

Verification of purchased product
The customer will be given access to examine goods and services that are purchased for incorporation their products, provided that our commercial secrets are not revealed.

We recognise that we are responsible for the level of quality in our company and that a customer's approval in such visits does not relieve us of our responsibilities.

Figure 6.9 Policy statement: verification of purchased product

SUMMARY

Suppliers must be assessed regularly for their overall level of service. The 'vendor assessment' system must be thorough and requires written procedures.

All goods/services purchased must be accurately specified in purchase orders. Reference to data sheets or specifications is expected.

The customer must be offered 'reasonable access' to inspect the goods/services purchased on their behalf. The customer's approval of these goods/services does not relieve you of your responsibility to achieve a high level of quality.

The policies for the three principal areas of the purchasing function (vendor assessment, purchasing data, verification) must be clearly stated, as control of incoming goods/services is an essential element of an effective quality assurance system.

Vendor assessment is a detailed examination system and requires exact procedures. It has been examined in depth in this module as it may not be familiar to all readers. The procedure(s) should refer to example documents (assessment sheets etc.).

The methods of purchasing should also be thoroughly specified in a procedure and referenced to the actual forms (purchase orders, requisition sheets etc.) in use.

Unless you have strict rules on allowing customers to view your office/factory, there is no need to define a procedure for such visits. Instead, the relevant policy statement can be satisfactory.

7

PURCHASER SUPPLIED PRODUCT

Goods/services supplied by your customer	ISO9001	ISO9002	ISO9003
	4.7	4.6	N/A

FUNCTION *In some businesses, customers may supply goods or services that are to be incorporated into the company's product. In these situations, the normal practice of vendor assessment is not applicable. Instead, other methods must be devised to maintain the level of quality.*

QUALITY MANAGEMENT

PURCHASER SUPPLIED PRODUCT As an example, in T. Bear Co., some customers supply packaging with their imprinted logo. On these orders, T. Bear use this material only, and the customer is required to supply a data sheet describing the quantity and specification of the packaging. This permits T. Bear to control the use of the product, ensuring that only correct grade packaging is used.

It is important to note that T. Bear are still obliged to produce a high quality packaged product for these customers. Normal standards of QA are not contravened. Thus they would still use their criteria to assess the suitability of the packaging, unless this was specifically excluded in their terms of contract.

The complexity of the policy and its associated procedure are dependent on the actual goods/services supplied and how you integrate it into your goods/services. Product liability and other legal responsibilities should be considered, particularly if the values of the supplied material are high.

Ultimately, it is your responsibility to ensure that the supplied product/service is of an acceptable grade. Where possible, you should

---

**T. Bear D & M Company
Purchaser supplied product**

If material is supplied by a customer for integration into our products to them, specific data on the quantity and quality of the material must be supplied.

The material will be processed and inspected according to our normal procedures, unless specified otherwise, in writing.

In all such cases where our procedures are not used, the general manager and management representative will first agree on alternative written procedures prior to using the material.

Procedures are used to describe our methods of handling purchaser supplied material.

Figure 7.1 Policy: purchaser supplied product

**T. Bear D & M Company
Purchaser supplied product – QA procedure**

All goods supplied by our customers for incorporation into their contracts with us are treated in the following manner.

1 The quantity and quality of the goods are checked on receipt and an advice note with these is forwarded to our customer.

2 In the event of any discrepancy between our assessment of quantity/ quality and the customer's delivery note, the customer is advised immediately. The QA manager is informed and will decide on the course of action.

3 The goods are labelled, identifying their contract reference number and the customer's name.

4 In the event of excess material being supplied, the customer is informed and will either remove the excess or permit us to store the goods for later use with their future contracts with us.

5 The excess material will only be used in customer's contracts and not in any other contract.

Figure 7.2 Procedure: purchaser supplied product

supply your specifications to the customer. This not only minimises problems, but can also lead to repeat business as the customer will be already familiar with your specifications. To meet the obligations of this section a few clear statements of your policy is required, as shown.

SUMMARY

Purchaser supplied materials must reach the same level of quality as those purchased from suppliers. Where such materials are used, they must be clearly identifiable and must not lower the quality of the normal output. Even though a customer may 'guarantee' suitability, it is your responsibility to maintain quality levels. This is of particular importance where product liability is concerned.

The policy statement can be brief and mainly states that you will accept customer supplied product. You should also clearly state that quality levels are your complete responsibility.

The procedures may also be short, principally describing the handling and testing of the supplied material.

8
PRODUCT IDENTIFICATION AND TRACEABILITY

Product identification and traceability	ISO9001	ISO9002	ISO9003
	4.8	4.7	4.4

FUNCTION *The raw materials or ingredients of a contract will go through numerous changes as they are processed into a final product. For example, foam has to be cut and shaped to fill the inside of T. Bear's toys and in the finished product is completely covered by an outer fabric.*

In a QA system, organised methods must be in place to permit identification of all materials at each stage of production. The identification process will allow you to follow the path of the raw materials through to their end use, this action being termed traceability.

QUALITY MANAGEMENT

PRODUCT IDENTIFICATION AND TRACEABILITY The necessity for identification of raw materials varies across industries and is dependent largely on the end use of the product. In the car and food industries a large proportion of the raw materials must be traceable, principally for reasons of safety. As an initial step towards addressing this module, consider your obligations to meet legislation, in particular safety law. Thereafter, your customers' requirements should be investigated. Identification and traceability systems can be very expensive and should be carefully designed. Generally, companies use these systems to meet legislation and to sieve out the sources of product failures.

Raw materials can be labelled in batches as they are processed and it is not necessary to identify uniquely every product manufactured unless there is a legal obligation. The policy statement can be brief

---

T. Bear D & M Company
Product identification and traceability

All raw materials are identified by identification and/or stock reference number as they are received in our goods inwards stores.

As materials are issued to the production line, they are primarily identified by description.

Where legislation or a contract stipulates identification of individual components, this is implemented and the use of each component recorded.

Figure 8.1 Policy: identification and traceability

and will reference the associated methods used, as shown in Figure 8.1. Note that industry practice and legislation should be your guiding lines to define the methods.

Associated procedures should include your methods of stock control, and the systems used for identification and traceability.

T. Bear D & M Company
Procedure – stock control

As goods are received, they are checked against the purchase order, and are then placed in our stores with a label identifying their description and part number.

Materials issued for production are labelled with a description only unless they are included on our material numbering list. This list contains those components and sub-assemblies that must be individually numbered, and the method for numbering and recording their use.

All certificates received with orders relating to goods purchased are given to the relevant buyer. These are stored with purchase orders.

The volume of stock is noted by adding goods received and deduction of goods issued from the initial stock volume. We maintain a list of the minimum volumes to be maintained for each raw material and order when we reach this volume.

A full inventory is taken every year and spot checks are made to ensure that we are maintaining accurate records.

Figure 8.2 Procedure: stock control

T. Bear D & M Company Procedure – labelling of finished products
All finished toys are labelled with the following identification marks on a white standard size No. 1 label. The company title. The product reference number. The safety legislation to which we have manufactured. The week and year number of manufacture. This label is affixed by stitching to the back of the toy and must be clearly legible to meet the requirements of our safety standard number xyz. The data outlined above are recorded in our finished product traceability register.

Figure 8.3 Procedure: identification – finished toys

SUMMARY

Materials from the raw component stage up to the completed product should be identifiable at all times. The degree of identification will rely on statutory legislation and industry practice. Where required, records are maintained indicating the use of the components and of the finished product. These records are termed traceability records.

The policy statement in Part 1 will refer to the obligations to meet legislation and contract requirements. It is a brief statement as the concepts of product identification and traceability are easily understood.

The procedures in Part 2 should include your stock control methods and separate methods to describe each type of identification/recording system used. Sample documents should be referenced and included in the appendices.

9
PROCESS CONTROL

Control of general and special processes in manufacturing, assembly and installation	ISO9001	ISO9002	ISO9003
	4.9	4.8	N/A

FUNCTION

After the design function, which has been previously addressed, come the manufacturing and installation functions. The definition and control of these elements of the business must be described in detail. Often, many of these procedures are already existing in the form of work method statements. The results of many manufacturing processes, painting for example, can be verified by testing methods and these are initially addressed. Thereafter those 'special' processes, welding for example, whose deficiencies only become apparent in use, are approached.

QUALITY MANAGEMENT

GENERAL

All work methods in manufacturing and installation must be specified in procedures or work instructions. They can address a particular process used across many products (painting for example) or a particular product (stitching a toy bear). They must be clear and precise, and must state what is regarded as a satisfactory level of quality. In particular, all customer requirements specified in the contracts must be honoured. Where possible, 'real' examples, models or photos, should be referenced. The policy statement will refer to the methods and also to the processes and equipment used by the staff. These processes and equipment must be suitable to carry out the required work, and should be approved by management.

SPECIAL PROCESSES

The previous processes addressed can be inspected and tested and, where found faulty, offending

---

T. Bear D & M Company
Process control

GENERAL

The production department operates through careful planning of customer contracts. Documented procedures and work instructions, detailed in Part 2, define the production and planning processes.

All production staff are responsible for the quality of their output and work in accordance with specified procedures. Where possible, actual samples of the level of quality expected are made available.

In addition, management staff are responsible for ensuring that all staff in their control are trained and able to produce quality output. Through regular training, all staff are made aware of the level of quality expected.

The production and planning function ensures that all work is carried out in a regular manner and that a clean, tidy production department is maintained.

Figure 9.1 Policy: process control – general

goods can be removed. However, this is not always the case. For scientific or economic reasons, there may be some 'special' processes whose faults only become apparent through use. In these situations, additional care must be taken in using the process, through monitoring and inspection. As previously advised in other modules, follow indus-

---

T. Bear D & M Company
Process control

SPECIAL PROCESSES

The company has identified the stitching of external fabrics as a special process, and operates rigorous procedures to control the process and testing methods. All relevant legislation is met and, where deemed necessary by the QA manager, external testing is carried out by approved testing laboratories.

This testing shall include non-destructive methods (X-ray) and destructive methods (tensioning of thread to breakage).

Figure 9.2 Policy: special processes

try practice. There are no specific rules on what should be considered a 'special process', other than that failure is usually exhibited over a period of use rather than through testing.

When you have identified your 'special processes', address them individually in the policy statement and in QA procedures and/or WIs as shown.

SUMMARY

The production and installation stages are described in QA procedures and WIs. Where possible, examples of satisfactory quality levels should be generally available to staff. Special processes are those whose deficiencies mainly show up over extended use. These require continuous monitoring and, from time to time, it is good practice to seek external professional advice in these areas.

The policy statement will refer separately to production and installation methods, including planning. Special processes require extensive monitoring and possibly external testing methods

The procedures and WIs should be extensive and refer to the desired quality level. Where possible, examples of the desired quality should be referenced and made available.

10
INSPECTION AND TESTING

Inspection and testing: receiving, in-process, final; records	ISO9001	ISO9002	ISO9003
	4.10	4.9	4.5

FUNCTION *Previously we have stated our policies and control methods for the design and manufacturing functions. We now address the inspection and testing carried out on the materials used in contracts.*

The materials are identified at three distinct stages in the company – upon receipt, during processing, as completed product – and are inspected at each stage. Finally, we address the maintenance of inspection and test records.

QUALITY MANAGEMENT

RECEIVING INSPECTION AND TESTING Materials must be inspected upon receipt to ensure that they meet the requirements of your purchase order. The degree of inspection must ensure that they are 'fit for use' and the verification methods are documented in procedures or in the quality plan. The supplier's reputation gained from vendor assessments, described in an earlier module, should be taken into account in deciding on the degree of inspection and test. The degree of certification supplied with the materials will also affect your decisions.

Sometimes material must be released into production without 'receiving inspection and test'. This material must be positively identified and noted to permit immediate recall should it cause problems at a later stage. This action is termed 'positive recall procedure', and should be specifically addressed in our policy and procedures.

T. Bear D & M Company
Inspection and testing

RECEIVING INSPECTION AND TESTING

All materials are inspected upon receipt and compared against our purchase order to ensure that they meet our requirements.

Certificates of conformance are inspected for accuracy and noted.

Materials that fail our inspection procedures are returned to the supplier and the QA manager notified.

Materials in our stores are classified and separated into three areas: awaiting inspection; passed inspection; rejected at inspection.

Under positive recall procedures, material issued without undergoing inspection and test is positively identified and noted.

Figure 10.1 Policy: receiving inspection and test

IN-PROCESS INSPECTION AND TEST The inspection and test methods carried out during processing are entirely industry dependent. However, as a general rule, inspect and test before and after the processes that bring the highest added value/costs as this will greatly reduce the value of reject material.

The procedures must verify that the parameters set in your process/product specifications are being achieved. Material issued under 'positive recall procedures' is now inspected with all other material. Should any of this material fail, it is usual practice to inspect all of the material issued under positive recall.

Material selected for inspection is placed 'on hold' until verified and production methods must take this into account. All non-conforming material must be identified and dealt with either by scrapping or reprocessing.

FINAL INSPECTION AND TEST At the end of the production process, a final inspection and test must be carried out to ensure that the goods meet specified requirements. These tests will include a check to ensure that all previous inspections (receiving and in-process) have been carried out successfully and documented correctly. The

---

T. Bear D & M Company
Company inspection and testing

IN-PROCESS INSPECTION AND TESTING

Throughout our manufacturing processes, random checks are carried out by management staff. These are in addition to the inspection and test points indicated in our general quality plan.

Where additional checks are specified in a contract, the QA manager will nominate personnel to carry out these tests.

All test results are recorded and all rejected material subject to further examination. This examination is carried out in order that we detect and eradicate the source of the problem causing material to be rejected.

Figure 10.2 Policy: in-process inspection and test

T. Bear D & M Company
Inspection and testing

FINAL INSPECTION AND TESTING

Upon completion of all manufacturing processes, functional and visual checks are carried out on all products using documented procedures.

All data gained from previous inspection and testing are cross-checked and random tests carried out for verification purposes.

Particular attention is paid to requirements of statutory legislation and, where necessary, all relevant tests and documentation completed.

The records of final inspection and test are reviewed daily by the management for accuracy, and to indicate any weaknesses in our procedures.

Figure 10.3 Policy: final inspection and test

final testing must ensure that the manufactured goods 'are fit for purpose' and must also be documented.

INSPECTION AND TEST RECORDS Throughout your inspection and testing, you will have generated numerous reports recording the results of your work. These records must be maintained as evidence

---

T. Bear D & M Company
Inspection and testing

INSPECTION AND TEST RECORDS

The records listed below which log the results of our inspection and testing are maintained. The method of maintenance is addressed in the Manual Section – Quality Records.

Goods Inwards Checklist and Copy of Purchase Order

In-Process Dimensional Checklists

Material Rejection Checklists

Final Inspection and Test Certificates

Figure 10.4 Policy: inspection and test records

of your inspection and testing procedures. A policy statement need simply mention the records that are maintained. There is no requirement for any QA procedures or WIs.

SUMMARY

Inspection and testing is carried out at three distinct stages in the company: upon receipt; during processing; at completed product. The primary function of inspection and testing is to ensure that the material used is at all times fit for purpose as defined in the specification. Failure to meet your specifications requires investigation of your methods and machinery to ensure that you remove the causes of failure.

Inspection and testing should be recorded as evidence of our material control system, and these records must be identified and maintained.

The three stages are addressed as outlined above, and are cross-referenced with their associated QAPs and WIs. No procedures are required relating to our records as all quality records are discussed in detail in a separate module.

11
INSPECTION, MEASURING AND TEST EQUIPMENT

Specification and calibration of inspection, test and measuring equipment	ISO9001	ISO9002	ISO9003
	4.11	4.10	4.6

FUNCTION

To ensure that your products meet your specified requirements, you must choose equipment to use in your testing. The equipment must also be calibrated and maintained to ensure test results are accurate. These selection and calibration methods are addressed in this module.

QUALITY MANAGEMENT

INSPECTION, MEASURING AND TEST EQUIPMENT

Common sense dictates that your requirements should not exceed your capabilities. However, you are obliged to check that you are meeting these requirements if you are to operate an effective QA system.

To do this, you need to assess your resources in design and manufacturing, and identify parameters that may be measured to indicate a given level of quality. You then select appropriate equipment that can measure these parameters. The policy statement, as shown in Figure 10.1, should simply refer to the fact that you establish such criteria.

When you have decided on the correct equipment, you must specify how to use it. This will include not only operating methods, but also calibration and maintenance procedures. Storage and handling of the equipment must also be specified. The calibration procedures will include the method of calibration and a record system to record the results of calibrations. These records provide evidence of your control system. Where required by contract, the records must be available to the customer, as shown on our example procedure.

T. Bear D & M Company
Inspection measuring and test equipment

The company operates procedures to ensure that our design and production personnel regularly review our specifications and identify the correct inspection, measuring and test equipment used to check conformance with these specifications.

Figure 11.1 Policy: use of procedures

T. Bear D & M Company
Inspection measuring and test equipment

The equipment selected for use is clearly identified and is made available to relevant staff who are trained in its operation. This training will include the method of safe storage and handling of the equipment.

Procedures are in operation regularly to maintain the accuracy of such equipment through systematic calibration methods. These methods, where possible, refer to international standards and the results of all calibrations are recorded.

Calibration records are made available to customers upon request to the QA manager, who has the sole authority to issue them to the public.

Figure 11.2 Policy: inspection, measuring and test

T. Bear D & M Company
Inspection measuring and test equipment

In the event that a piece of equipment is found to be out of calibration, the QA manager is immediately notified.

Where safety may be jeopardised, all products remaining in our company are rechecked against the recalibrated equipment and our normal testing procedures carried out. Those products that are outside our company will be recalled.

Figure 11.3 Policy: inspection, measuring and test

Finally you must address what happens when you discover that a piece of equipment is out of calibration. Depending on your industry this will have varying significance. Statutory obligations must be honoured, particularly where product safety is required. A brief statement of your actions is all that is required.

SUMMARY

The methods of selection and using inspection, measuring and test equipment are addressed, including maintenance of associated records. The use and calibration of equipment is documented in specific procedures that reference the relevant equipment calibration/maintenance manuals.

Our policy of selection, use and maintenance of equipment is in Part 1. These can be general with all specific methods referred to in the QA procedures and WIs. A systematic calibration system is required to meet the requirements of the ISO9000 standards.

12
INSPECTION AND TEST STATUS

Inspection and test status of materials; labeling of status	ISO9001	ISO9002	ISO9003
	4.12	4.11	4.7

FUNCTION   *The inspection and test status of all material must be clearly identified. Our aim is to ensure that only 'passed' material reaches the customer. All other material will be scrapped or reworked. Methods of identifying the status of material are addressed in this module.*

QUALITY MANAGEMENT

INSPECTION AND TEST STATUS   The policy states the methods of identification which are clarified in QA procedures/WIs. The status of material can be indicated either by labelling or simply by its physical position. For example, you can allocate space in your stores

---

**T. Bear D & M Company
Inspection and test status**

All reject and scrap material is clearly identified and placed in containers.

The inspection and test reports for all products are checked prior to dispatch to ensure that all material meets specification. Dispatch documents are only released after this final inspection.

The inspection and test reports are at all times signed by the personnel carrying out this work.

Failure to meet the above requirements will result in the material not progressing through our company and it will be placed 'on hold' for further inspection and testing.

Figure 12.1 Policy: inspection and test status

to 'untested' and 'passed' parts by simply placing the parts in different boxes (the boxes must be labelled), or by placing on separately
labelled shelving. Reject or scrap material must be clearly separated
from all other material to prevent accidental use.

SUMMARY

Material in the company must be clearly identified to distinguish its
status during inspection and testing. As the details of inspection and
test, including the use of associated equipment, are addressed in separate modules, this section of the manual can be brief.

The short policy statement outlined is acceptable, provided the
inspection function is clearly addressed. Procedures in Part 2 should
refer to appropriate labelling or segregation of material. It is not
necessary to use expensive or bureaucratic control methods.
Simplicity of operation is essential.

13
CONTROL OF
NONCONFORMING PRODUCT

Control of reject, reworked, low quality and scrap material	ISO9001	ISO9002	ISO9003
	4.13	4.12	4.8

FUNCTION *Material that has failed to pass the inspection and testing stages must be isolated. This material will then be either reworked, scrapped or sold, depending on company policy. The methods of controlling 'failed' or 'nonconforming' material are addressed in this module.*

QUALITY MANAGEMENT

GENERAL A brief introductory policy statement stating that you have procedures to deal with nonconforming product is all that is required as shown below.

NONCONFORMITY REVIEW AND DISPOSITION The details of how to deal with nonconforming material are now addressed. First

---

T. Bear D & M Company
Control of nonconforming product

The company operates procedures to ensure adequate control of all material that fails to meet our specifications. These procedures prevent such material being used or sent to our customers.

The procedures ensure that such material is identified, segregated, noted and disposed with in a consistent way.

Figure 13.1 Policy: nonconforming product

T. Bear D & M Company **Control of nonconforming product**
NONCONFORMITY REVIEW AND DISPOSITION The company's procedures ensure that nominated staff will review all actions taken regarding nonconforming material. The review will address all relevant information and decide on a course of action which will determine if the material is: 1 reprocessed to meet our requirements; or 2 accepted for use with or without rework after permission has been received by the customer; or 3 used for an alternative purpose for which it is suitable; or 4 rejected completely and scrapped. In all cases the material will be clearly identified and reinspected to meet our requirements where required. The actions taken will be recorded and, where appropriate, the actions for rework etc. noted on instructions to personnel.

Figure 13.2 Policy: nonconformity review and disposition

of all, it must be established who will make decisions regarding the disposal of the product, and this, in most cases, will be a senior member of staff. Then you should consider the different options open, regarding disposal of the material. You should record both the occurrence and actions taken to deal with the nonconforming material. Where obliged by law, particularly in the food industry, or contract you must also inform your customers.

The example in Figure 13.2 shows the usual options regarding disposal of material. These are specifically mentioned in the standards and should be addressed. It also addresses your contract obligations and a specific point raised in the standards – that you must inform the customer if you use or repair nonconforming material in their contract.

The procedures for carrying out inspection and testing are referenced, and a specific procedure regarding nonconforming product should be written as shown in Figure 13.3.

T. Bear D & M Company
Procedure – nonconforming product

Purpose
To define our methods used to control nonconforming product.

Methods
1 The goods inwards officer will raise all Nonconforming Reports (SD5) where materials on receipt fail to meet our requirements.

2 These are passed to the Chief Buyer and QA Manager who will decide on a course of action.

3 Where goods are rejected, the supplier will be sent a copy of the nonconforming report and required to replace the material. This will also be noted in the supplier's Vendor Assessment File.

4 Where a material, in-process or at final inspection and test, fails to meet our requirements, the Production Supervisor will Raise the Nonconforming Report (SD5).

5 These are passed to the Chief Buyer and QA Manager who will decide on a course of action.

6 The course of action will be described on a Nonconforming Material Action Report which will be given to the Production Supervisor for action.

7 Where a customer concession is required the QA Manager will contact the customer and seek their permission, in writing, to use the material.

Figure 13.3 Procedure: nonconforming product

SUMMARY

The methods used to deal with material that fails to meet your specifications must be clearly stated. These must identify the faulty material and the staff who decide on a course of action. This course of action is documented, including the relevant documents that must be used.

The policy must address the four options open to deal with nonconforming material and the question of customer concessions.

Procedures referenced should include relevant inspection and test methods, and a specific procedure to define your actions concerning control of nonconforming product.

14
CORRECTIVE ACTION

Customer complaints; analyses of inspection and test failures; corrective measures	ISO9001	ISO9002	ISO9003
	4.14	4.13	N/A

FUNCTION *When you produce a faulty product or receive a customer complaint, it is usually an indication of some fault in your company QA system. Possible faults might be a badly written inspection and testing procedure or faulty equipment that has not been detected, for example. Whatever the cause, you need methods to investigate these problems that will conclude with suggestions for remedial action. These methods are addressed in this module and include a customer complaints procedure. The complaints procedure is explained in detail in this module.*

QUALITY MANAGEMENT

CORRECTIVE ACTION The policy statement separately addresses a number of areas mentioned in the standard. In our example, they are addressed in the following sequence.

1 We are obliged to investigate the causes of producing nonconforming product and to provide remedial action to prevent recurrence. This effectively means analysing the reports generated when we detect nonconforming product and then sourcing the faults.

2 All processes and related procedures and records generated by our QA system should be analysed for weaknesses that may cause us to produce nonconforming product. Any weakness detected should be remedied. These records include service reports and customer complaints.

3 We must use preventive action in proportion to the level of risk met. This will mean analysing our business products for possible sources of faults and applying methods to prevent faults occurring. Failure mode and effects analysis (FMEA) is one of the 'tools' used by some larger businesses to prevent low quality produce. It involves investigating the cause and possible effects of hypothetical product or process failures. (The topic of FMEA is beyond the scope of this book. For further detail on implementation, seek professional advice.)

4 We must use methods to control our use of corrective action and to ensure that they are effective. Essentially this means checking our corrective methods for practicality, to ensure a quick but economic solution in correcting faults.

5 Finally, we must implement and record the changes that occur in our procedures resulting from corrective action. This will invariably refer to our document control procedures.

The policy below mentions the use of customer complaints procedures, which are required in all businesses for QA purposes. There follows a brief summary of such a system.

T. Bear D & M Company
Corrective action

The company operates procedures that involve regular review of all records generated by our system, plus other records that the QA manager chooses. Any trends are investigated and appropriate remedial action taken.

All procedures are regularly reviewed with a view to improvement that will lower our risk of producing nonconforming material.

Management and other staff nominated by management attend these review meetings.

The corrective actions are also analysed for effectiveness and appropriate changes made to our method of analysis if required.

Where necessary, procedures are altered and recorded as a result of this corrective action.

Figure 14.1 Policy: corrective action

All customer complaints should be investigated to detect and elimi-nate potential causes of low quality. Complaints are often hard to categorise and validate, but in most cases indicate a weakness in the company. Complaints can also be hard to identify, as a simple criti-cism about the company might not be registered as a formal complaint by the customer.

If we take a complaint and analyse it, it can be broken up into a number of elements such as date received, source of complaint, con-tent etc. It can be helpful to categorise the complaint further into the degree of remedial action required, or into the product or service referred to.

What an effective complaint system must demonstrate is a logging system to store complaint records, and an orderly procedure to action and resolve the complaint. It must also ensure that the cause of the complaint is resolved internally in the company to minimise it occur-ring in future. The actual methods to log and investigate complaints are recorded as a work instruction or QA procedure.

Figure 14.2 gives an example of a complaint form used to register complaints. A QA procedure defining the methods used in investigat-ing complaints is detailed in the QA manual in Part 2 of this book.

In designing your own complaints procedure and associated forms it is best to put yourself in the position of your customer. The complaints system must be rigorous but must not deter a customer from complain-ing or overburdening your own company with useless detail. The detailed complaint form shown in Figure 14.3 contains just enough detail to identify the customer, the complaint and the follow-up actions.

SUMMARY

Our corrective actions must be clear and not only refer to past errors, but also investigate the risk of other future errors. All the corrective actions should themselves be checked for effectiveness. Any changes in procedures resulting from the corrective action should be docu-mented and implemented.

The policy outlined will satisfy all three requirements. The proce-dures in Part 2 should include a specific method of remedying customer complaints and our method of analysing our quality performance.

Date: 23/11/XX	Complaint Number: TB 09	
Name: J. Bloggs	Form of complaint: Letter	Received by: Salesman
Complaint	There was a shortage of bears in the recent delivery which resulted in lost sales and profit. He wants to know if he will receive a discount with the next order.	
Reply	Required by marketing department.	
Actioned	24/11/9X *Marketing Department – T. Bloggs* Investigation shows that his order was misread by the dispatch department. As he is a regular customer we will give him 10% discount on next order	
Reviewed	Marketing and dispatch departments reviewed the matter at the complaints meeting of 1/12/9X and have suggested a new format for the order form. The customer is now happy with our service.	

Figure 14.2 Basic customer complaint form

	CUSTOMER COMPLAINT FORM	
T. Bear Design & Manufacturing	COMPLAINT NO: TB/04	
	NAME: JOE BLOGGS ADDRESS: UNIT 2067 THE FIRS	
	LOGGING DATE: 19/11/9X	CONTACT: J. BLOGGS
FORM OF COMPLAINT	LETTER OF 19/11/9X	
RECEIVED BY	*SALES DEPARTMENT – T. BLOGGS*	
NATURE OF COMPLAINT	SHORTAGE OF BEARS IN RECENT DELIVERY. WANTS A DISCOUNT ON NEXT ORDER BECAUSE OF LOST PROFIT AND COSTS INCURRED BY HIM IN PROMOTING OUR PRODUCTS.	
PRODUCTS MENTIONED	BEARS – CHRISTMAS STYLE	
REPLY REQUIRED	WRITTEN – BY MARKETING DEPARTMENT	
TARGET DATE TO RESOLVE	URGENT – 20/11/9X	
ACTION	DISPATCHED REMAINDER OF HIS ORDER 5/333GE ON 20/11/9X AT 10% DISCOUNT – LETTER OF APOLOGY SENT 20/11/9X BY T. BLOGGS	
RESOLVED	SATISFACTORILY – CUSTOMER WILL REMAIN LOYAL	
REVIEWED	COMPLAINTS COMMITTEE 23/11/9X. SHORTAGE WAS DUE TO RAW MATERIAL DAMAGED IN TRAN-SIT WHICH RESULTED IN LOST PRODUCTION	
STATUS	RESOLVED	

Figure 14.3 Typical customer complaint form

15
HANDLING, STORAGE, PACKAGING AND DELIVERY

Specification of methods and documents used in the final handling of products and delivery to customers	ISO9001	ISO9002	ISO9003
	4.15	4.14	4.9

> FUNCTION

After final inspection, the product is packaged and delivered. Prior to delivery, the product may be stored awaiting dispatch. These elements of contract requirements are now addressed. The policy statement need only mention that these final steps are recognised. As in prior modules, the individual work methods used in handling, storage, packaging and delivery are addressed in procedures.

QUALITY MANAGEMENT

> GENERAL

The general statement mentions that procedures regarding handling, storage, packaging and delivery are in place. These elements are then addressed later.

> HANDLING

The handling of materials must ensure that loss or damage does not occur. This will include the use

---

T. Bear D & M Company
Handling, storage, packaging and delivery

GENERAL

The company operates procedures to protect the finished products from damage or loss during handling, storage, packaging and delivery.

Figure 15.1 Policy: general comment

of safe and clean methods to move the material, with relevant staff receiving training where necessary.

T. Bear D & M Company Handling, storage, packaging and delivery
HANDLING
All materials are handled with care to prevent any damage. Through experience, we have developed methods to ensure careful and safe movement of materials throughout our company. Managers ensure that staff are adequately trained in the handling of materials.

Figure 15.2 Policy: material handling

STORAGE

Storage areas must be set aside during all the stages of receiving, processing and dispatching the finished product. The material must be clearly identified and stored in a clean and safe area. In addition, storage methods should define the method of stock rotation, where this is important to your industry (e.g. food industry). Any staff with specific responsibilities in the area should be identified.

T. Bear D & M Company Handling, storage, packaging and delivery
STORAGE
The company ensures that adequate areas are set aside for materials from receipt at goods inwards to final dispatch.
All materials are clearly identified, and are stored in proper racks and containers. Where necessary, storage is provided in controlled temperature environments as with any inflammable materials.
Relevant staff are trained in storage methods and periodic checks are carried out to ensure our procedures are used correctly.

Figure 15.3 Policy: material storage

PACKAGING All materials must have adequate protection from damage. Where necessary, such as with fragile items, specialised packaging may be required. The actual type of packaging can be specified in data sheets if necessary and need only be referred to in your procedure.

T. Bear D & M Company
Handling, storage, packaging and delivery

PACKAGING

All material is packaged with suitable protection where necessary. The packaging is designed to prevent damage and to display identity labels that are affixed to our products. Where a customer's packaging requirements are stipulated in a contract these are met completely and shall not be of a lower standard than our usual packaging. Relevant staff are trained to use the packaging equipment in a safe manner.

Figure 15.4 Policy: material packaging

DELIVERY The delivery of the packaged products must be organised to ensure that the correct product arrives safely, without damage and on time at the customer's location. Additionally, it must be ensured that all relevant documentation, including any certificates and delivery notes, accompanies each consignment. The types of documents will be found in your procedures and in the contract requirements. The policy statement need only be brief.

T. Bear D & M Company
Handling, storage, packaging and delivery

DELIVERY

Dispatch documents identifying the destination and sufficient detail to identify the contract and product are forwarded with each consignment. All reasonable effort is made to ensure that the product is delivered safely and undamaged with the required documents.

Where necessary, these will include specific handling procedures.

Figure 15.5 Policy: delivery

SUMMARY

This module addresses the final steps in completing your customer contracts. The areas of handling, storage, packaging and delivery of finished product are discussed in one policy statement, referring to the appropriate procedures.

The policy statement should address each area individually, referring to relevant personnel where possible. It is best to be as brief as possible and leave all detail in the procedures.

The procedures should address your method of stock control, as this concerns storage and handling. Specific description of shelving for storage is not required unless you are in a highly specialised industry (e.g. clean rooms in electronic industry). If specific materials are used in packaging, treat these as specification sheets. This will reduce the amount of re-editing in the manual when you change specifications.

Checklists indicating the different types of documentation required by your customers will prove particularly helpful.

16
QUALITY RECORDS

Maintenance and storage of quality records	ISO9001	ISO9002	ISO9003
	4.16	4.15	4.10

FUNCTION *Throughout the quality assurance system, numerous different types of records have been defined and referred to. This module concerns the approach to maintenance and storage of these records.*

QUALITY MANAGEMENT

QUALITY RECORDS Your policy statement must address the following topics concerning quality records:

identification;
collection;
indexing;
filing;
storage;
maintenance;
disposal.

Previous modules have addressed many of these topics already. Here, it is sufficient to state our policy briefly and provide a graphical explanation as in the later example. A QA procedure is not required unless you happen to have a complicated method of storage (off-site for example).

A policy should take into account any legal obligations, particularly regarding consumer and personnel legislation. Many countries now have laws governing storage of personnel data in computers. If in doubt about your obligations, contact your State department for industry.

In a policy statement, it is good practice to identify the holder of the documents. Where confidentiality is required, the 'holders' must be chosen with care. Finally, note that although the style of records varies from company to company, all companies must maintain the records identified in the QA system. The example in Figure 16.2 is an extract and does not contain all the record types.

T. Bear D & M Company Quality records
The company maintains records created within the QA system which record the operation of our system.
The records are created by relevant personnel at the times required by our procedures and are representative of the level of quality achieved.
All records are available to pertinent staff and are arranged in an easily retrievable manner. Where possible, records are stored in a place convenient to their use and in a suitable environment. Confidential records are of limited access.
Records are held for at least the retention period specified.

Figure 16.1 Policy: quality records

Quality records – management system			
RECORD TYPE	INDEXING METHOD	OFFICIAL HOLDER	RETENTION PERIOD
MANAGEMENT REVIEW REPORTS	DATE	QA MANAGER	5 YEARS
PURCHASE ORDERS	NUMERICAL	BUYER	5 YEARS
APPROVED SUPPLIER LISTS	DATE	QA MANAGER	5 YEARS
CONTRACTS	NUMERICAL/ YEAR	SALES MANAGER	10 YEARS
ETC.			

Figure 16.2 Quality records maintenance

SUMMARY

The quality records generated by your system must be collated and easily retrievable. Many records will have to be retained for a number of years. The details outlined regarding record maintenance are both easy and cost little to adhere to. With the great increase in personal computer use, it is relatively cheap to set up a retrieval system using a database package. The use of software in the management of quality is discussed separately in this book.

17
INTERNAL QUALITY AUDITS

Systematic review and audit of QA management system	ISO9001	ISO9002	ISO9003
	4.17	4.16	N/A

FUNCTION *A QA system contains many procedures and methods used to manage a business. As mentioned earlier in the book, these must be reviewed and updated frequently to reflect change. These reviews only affect individual elements and not the overall operation of the system. To get an overall view of the system its operation must also be investigated. This inspection is termed an internal quality audit and it must be carried out regularly.*

QUALITY MANAGEMENT

INTERNAL QUALITY AUDITS The function of the quality audit is to measure actual operation of the QA system as opposed to planned operation. The overall efficiency and adequacy must be investigated. To gain an impartial and alternative view, staff not directly involved in a procedure should check its operation. (These staff should, however, have a broad understanding of the topics under investigation, gained from either previous experience or training.)

All quality related activities are audited, the frequency and depth of audit reflecting the importance of the activity within your QA system. As both procedures and their relevance are checked, the quality audits form an important element of the QA system. In many ways they are similar to the vendor assessment function described earlier, where suppliers were audited.

It is usual that a standard reporting method or form is used during auditing, ensuring that specified topics are addressed and that a consistent level of auditing is achieved in the long term. All audits and subsequent actions must be documented, as is the audit procedure itself.

Usual practice is that the results of audits are brought to the attention of all relevant senior personnel as quickly as possible after the audit. The senior management will address the results of these audits at internal management reviews as described in Module 1 (Management Responsibility). The example policy statement in Figure 17.1 addresses each of these points. In Figure 17.2, there is an example procedure detailing the methods of systematically auditing a QA system.

The procedure addresses who will carry out the audits, when they are carried out and the method of addressing any problems shown in the audits. A sample auditing form, to be completed by each auditor, is also shown in Figure 17.3.

T. Bear D & M Company
Internal quality audits

Internal quality audits are carried out to check that we are following procedures and to assess their effectiveness.

The QA manager designs an audit schedule to ensure that all quality related activities are audited at least annually.

The quality reports (SD8) are reviewed by the QA manager and the quality management review team, and appropriate corrective action taken.

Figure 17.1 Policy: internal quality audits

SUMMARY

Quality system audits are a method of checking that a QA system is being adhered to and that it is relevant. The complete QA system should be reviewed regularly and on a systematic basis.

Any nonconformances must be indicated and senior management informed. Corrective action must then be noted and the element reaudited, if necessary, to ensure compliance.

The above may all be addressed generally in a policy statement, with a specific procedure given for carrying out internal quality audits in the procedures manual.

T. Bear D & M Company **Procedure – internal quality audits**
Purpose To ensure that our company is adhering to the policies and methods in the quality manual, and to detect areas of improvement in our QA system. *Methods* The QA manager prepares an audit schedule defining the frequency of auditing for each element of our system. All elements of the system are audited at least annually. Where noncompliance with our system has been detected, those elements are audited monthly until operating consistently to our procedures over two audits. Staff nominated by the QA manager carry out the audits. The results of audits, completed on our system audit form (SD7) are available to all supervisory staff in the relevant area. Senior management review the audit reports regularly and decide on appropriate corrective action. All corrective action is recorded and, where a contract stipulates, the audit report forms are made available to the customer. Records are maintained for a period of five years.

Figure 17.2 Procedure: internal quality audits

	SYSTEM AUDIT FORM – SD4	
T. Bear Design & Manufacturing	AUDIT NO.:	
	AUDITOR:	
	DATE:	ISO9001 REF:

SUBJECT UNDER AUDIT:	
ITEM	COMMENT

OVERALL COMMENT:

CONFORMS TO STANDARD: YES/NO

SIGNED:

Figure 17.3 Example system audit form (Apx)

18
TRAINING

Staff training systems and records	ISO9001	ISO9002	ISO9003
	4.18	4.17	4.11

FUNCTION	*Staff and workforce must be properly trained to carry out the company business. Activities demand-*

ing acquired skills must be identified and the necessary training provided. The skills required in the business are obvious in many cases and often determined by regulations or industry practice. Some skills required may be less obvious and require identification. This module addresses the policy statement and an associated method of recording training skills. Methods of identifying skill requirements and training schemes for staff are addressed.

QUALITY MANAGEMENT

TRAINING	Every employee, to a greater or lesser extent, affects the quality level of your company.

Training records provide a simple tool to identify and develop the strengths and weaknesses of staff. They are easy to construct, as frequently the information is known, if not documented.

Your policy statement should simply address your method of approaching the training function. A QA procedure is used to describe specific methods of training staff and recording the relevant details. This will also include the approach to skill identification and training.

The statement is brief and refers to the intention to train all staff to be able to carry out their job function. The types of training record used should also be addressed, as shown.

T. Bear D & M Company Training
The company operates procedures to ensure that all staff are trained to carry out work to meet our contract requirements.
Staff are selected based on their aptitude and ability to carry out their work.
All staff are encouraged to develop their skills and adequate training courses and funds are made available.
The company maintains staff training records which are regularly reviewed and updated as appropriate. Any shortage of skills is noted and either new staff hired or existing staff trained.

Figure 18.1 Policy: training

TRAINING RECORDS As a first step to establishing training records, for just three employees, list the training or abilities that each one has, using the example in Figure 18.2.

Name: Joe Bloggs	Task
Ability under supervision	Sewing, stuffing
Ability unsupervised	Sealing
Requires full training	--------------------

Figure 18.2 Basic training record

Now draw a grid of vertical and horizontal lines. List the employees horizontally and the current work specifications vertically. Transfer your data from the three records as shown in Figure 18.3.

You have now the basic concepts to establish a training record system for your company. To establish a usable set of records, there must be methods to define the work (these are usually defined in work instructions and quality assurance procedures) and a method to identify the associated employees. It is helpful if the grid can categorise the actual ability of employees as indicated by supervised, unsupervised, unable etc., but do not make the grid too complex.

	Sewing	Stuffing	Sealing
Joe Bloggs	Supervised	Supervised	Unsupervised
Jim Bloggs	Requires full training	Supervised	Requires full training
John Bloggs	Unsupervised	Requires full training	Unsupervised

Figure 18.3 A basic 'workability' grid

Where appropriate, competence should be demonstrated by in-house or external testing. In everyday business, all too often the competence of staff is taken for granted. This can result in the wrong staff being selected to carry out work, resulting in poor work or loss of business. In addition, weaknesses in staff training can lead to lost opportunities, while a small investment in training may lead to increased business.

Often staff will have 'unique' abilities and these can be ignored if you form too tight a work specification. You might happily be meeting the requirements of the QA standards, but omitting valuable business information. In these cases, simply add a memo to that person's training records. In addition, try to attach a record of training costs to each record. These are not currently required by the ISO standards, but are a useful tool for the manager to use for financial budgeting purposes.

SUMMARY

Training records defining the ability of staff to carry out their work are required to comply with the ISO standards. These indicate the level of ability relevant to each WI/QA procedure. In addition, they should contain as much valuable information as possible, such as attendance on training courses etc.

The records should be maintained regularly and preferably by the same management team. Like all personnel records they should remain confidential, this being a legal obligation in many countries.

 **T. Bear** Design & Manufacturing	**STAFF TRAINING RECORD**
	EMPLOYEE NO.: DESIGN/04
	NAME: JOE BLOGGS
	DATE: 20/6/9X REV: 2

ABILITY	TASK
SUPERVISED	WI 23 REV2 – SEWING OF LARGE PANDAS
	WI 24 REV0 – SEWING OF SMALL TOY RANGE
UNSUPERVISED	WI 09 REV2 – INSPECTION OF SMALL TOY RANGE
	WI 12 REV2 – FILLING OF LARGE CHRISTMAS BEAR
	WI 14 REV2 – FILLING OF SMALL TOY RANGE
AUDIT	WI 80 REV3 – AUDIT OF SUPPLIERS OF FILLING AND OUTER FABRIC
NOTES	REQUIRES SOME TRAINING TO FULLY UNDERSTAND VENDOR ASSESSMENT AND ITS PRINCIPLES. IS INTERESTED IN PRODUCT DEVELOPMENT
COURSES	HAS ATTENDED FOUR INTERNAL TRAINING COURSES IN JUNIOR MANAGEMENT – INTERNAL COURSES 1–4

Figure 18.4 A completed training record (Apx)

19
SERVICING

Servicing and maintenance agreements with customers	ISO9001	ISO9002	ISO9003
	4.19	N/A	N/A

FUNCTION *The types of servicing/maintenance/guarantee agreements existing between customer and supplier vary greatly over industry. To address servicing through your QA system, you must have procedures and controls to verify the level of quality achieved. Your policy statement again should contain your objectives, while the associated procedures are prepared separately.*

QUALITY MANAGEMENT

SERVICING The servicing module can be approached in the same way as the subject of process control. Our example revolves around a repair unit within our production department that repairs old toys. Our contracts are to repair product that is no longer covered under warranty.

Our work methods are again specified in procedures used by our staff to carry out the repairs.

The level and type of service arrangement will depend on our contractual obligations and local legislation. When servicing is carried out for safety reasons, it is often a requirement that the work and recording methods are agreed in advance of the work being carried out, with insurance and/or government agencies. In these situations, seek professional advice as any mistakes can prove very costly.

With increasing competition and improved quality of manufacture, guarantee periods are now much longer than they were a few years ago. This also means that records must be maintained for longer periods and it is not unusual to retain records for ten years in many industries.

T. Bear D & M Company
Servicing

The servicing department operates to carry out repairs on toys no longer covered by warranty.

Our procedures used ensure that we carry out our work to a high level of quality and in a speedy manner.

Through old catalogues and samples we attempt to repair old products back to their original state.

Management staff are responsible for ensuring that all staff are adequately trained and aware of the level of quality expected.

Scheduling is carried out by the production department under which the servicing operates.

Figure 19.1 Policy: servicing

As with the 'process control' module, all related work procedures must be defined clearly. Methods of inspection and test to ensure that the servicing is correct will often be those used already during manufacture.

SUMMARY

Servicing varies greatly according to industry and your methods should at least meet industry practice. The methods and records of servicing must honour both your contractual obligations and any relevant legislation.

Service records are usually maintained for longer periods than most other records in your QA system. Software methods applicable are discussed separately in this book.

Analysis of these records can prevent future product failures and it is common practice to review service records at least every three months.

20
STATISTICAL TECHNIQUES

Statistical methods to measure and control quality	ISO9001	ISO9002	ISO9003
	4.20	4.18	4.12

FUNCTION *Statistical methods are widely used in manufacturing industry to control processes and to select material according to particular characteristics. The use and application of statistical methods is addressed in this final module. There is a vast range of methods and applications of statistics, and the reader is advised to seek professional advice before introducing statistical techniques.*

QUALITY MANAGEMENT

STATISTICAL METHODS The use of statistical methods in industry is mainly concentrated in material testing and process control. On a simplistic level, the methods involve taking samples of material or output at regular intervals. Through analysing the samples, the 'quality' of the process is measured and, if necessary, altered to maintain a target level of quality.

To measure 'quality', you must first of all set *achievable* parameters that you will measure, and then define methods of measurement. Your frequency of measurement and the methods of analysis must also be defined. It is here that professional advice is required, as incorrect application of statistical methods will, at the very least, prove a useless exercise and can be very expensive.

It is probable that your customers will be able to assist in defining the statistical methods to use, as they are largely dependent on industry. Hi-tech electronic industries, where reliability is extremely important, use statistical methods a great deal, while industries where reliability is not of such a high standard, and repair costs are low, rarely use them.

To meet the requirements of the standards, you are only obliged to follow industry practice and this should be your guideline. For many small industries, it is satisfactory to simply carry out random sampling of product during different manufacturing stages and to grade these for acceptance or rejection. The sampling procedure defined in a QA procedure can be simple as in our example. Although referring to our toy company, it was derived from a real QA manual for a small engineering company.

T. Bear D & M Company
Statistical techniques

The company operates statistical procedures in accordance with the terms of each customer contract. These sampling procedures are principally used at inspection of raw materials and prior to final dispatch.

In the absence of procedures being specified by the customer contract, the company operates to the general principle of the sampling techniques most commonly used in the customer's country.

Records of all statistical procedures are maintained and forwarded to the customer where necessary.

Figure 20.1 Policy statistical techniques

SUMMARY

Statistical techniques vary from industry to industry and external advice should be used prior to introducing a statistical sampling system. The use of statistics is a *science* and incorrect use will prove costly. Contrary to popular opinion, it is not a requirement to operate detailed statistical procedures and many companies make little use of statistical techniques, but readily meet the requirements of the ISO standards.

QUALITY ASSURANCE MANUAL PART 1

QA policies

TABLE OF CONTENTS

QUALITY ASSURANCE POLICIES

ISSUE DATE: 1/12/9X   ISSUE #:1

TITLE	ISSUE DATE	ISSUE	PAGES	REF
Management responsibility	1/12/9X	1	6	1
Quality system	1/12/9X	2	2	2
Contract review	1/12/9X	1	1	3
Design control	1/12/9X	1	2	4
Document control	1/12/9X	1	1	5
Purchasing	1/12/9X	1	2	6
Purchaser supplied product	1/12/9X	1	1	7
Product identification and traceability	1/12/9X	1	1	8
Process control	1/12/9X	1	2	9
Inspection and testing	1/12/9X	1	3	10
Inspection, measuring and test equipment	1/12/9X	1	1	11
Inspection and test status	1/12/9X	1	1	12
Control of nonconforming product	1/12/9X	1	1	13
Corrective action	1/12/9X	1	1	14
Handling, storage, packaging and delivery	1/12/9X	1	2	15
Quality records	1/12/9X	1	2	16
Internal quality records	1/12/9X	1	1	17
Training	1/12/9X	1	1	18
Servicing	1/12/9X	1	1	19
Statistical techniques	1/12/9X	1	1	20

T. BEAR DESIGN & MANUFACTURING	ISSUE #: 1
PART 1: SECTION 1	ISSUE DATE: 1/12/9X
SUBJECT: MANAGEMENT RESPONSIBILITY	PAGE 1 OF 6

1.1 QUALITY POLICY

1.1.1 It is the policy of T. Bear Design & Manufacturing Company to design and manufacture toy bears at an economic level to standards and design requirements of our customers. All relevant safety requirements are met. In addition, our policy is to monitor our work regularly to ensure that our quality objectives are met.

1.1.2 In our company we have prepared a quality manual which contains the company's policies and procedures relating to quality.

1.1.3 All staff are obliged to adhere to the procedures in the quality manual.

1.1.4 Employees and our customers are encouraged to make suggestions that will improve our level of quality.

1.1.5 Our company is at present operating to the objectives of the ISO Standard 9001. Our suppliers are encouraged to operate similar systems.

1.1.6 This manual refers to our London site only. All products designed and manufactured there meet the requirements of this manual.

Signed: J. BLOGGS, CHIEF EXECUTIVE OFFICER

T. BEAR DESIGN & MANUFACTURING	ISSUE #: 1
PART 1: SECTION 1	ISSUE DATE: 1/12/9X
SUBJECT: MANAGEMENT RESPONSIBILITY	PAGE 2 OF 6

1.2 ORGANISATION

1.2.1 Responsibility and Authority

The company management organisation is shown in Figure 1 attached. Job descriptions are in Appendix 1.

1.2.2 Verification Resources and Personnel

The company QA function is shown in Figure 2 attached. The QA manager is the 'management representative' as described in section 1.2.3 below.

In each department staff, selected by the QA manager, are responsible for checking the departmental inputs and outputs. These functions include:

checking drawings and calculations in the drawing department;

inspection of the materials purchased;

inspection of the product as it is under manufacture;

calibration of test equipment.

Staff receive specific training where necessary.

1.2.3 Management Representative

The company has appointed a QA manager to implement the company's policies towards QA. This person has full responsibility and authority in all QA related matters and reports directly to the company chief executive officer.

The duties of the QA manager include:

T. BEAR DESIGN & MANUFACTURING	ISSUE #: 1
PART 1: SECTION 1	ISSUE DATE: 1/12/9X
SUBJECT: MANAGEMENT RESPONSIBILITY	PAGE 3 OF 6

ensuring that our QA system complies with ISO9001;

maintenance and revision of the manual;

co-ordination with external advisers in development of our QA system.

T. BEAR DESIGN & MANUFACTURING	ISSUE #: 1
PART 1: SECTION 1	ISSUE DATE: 1/12/9X
SUBJECT: MANAGEMENT RESPONSIBILITY	PAGE 4 OF 6

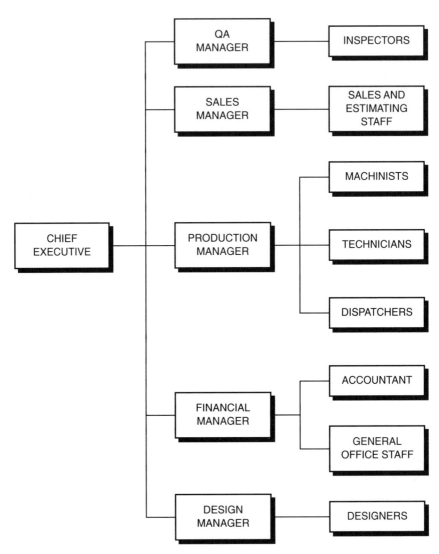

Figure 8: Company management structure (outline)

T. BEAR DESIGN & MANUFACTURING	ISSUE #: 1
PART 1: SECTION 1	ISSUE DATE: 1/12/9X
SUBJECT: MANAGEMENT RESPONSIBILITY	PAGE 5 OF 6

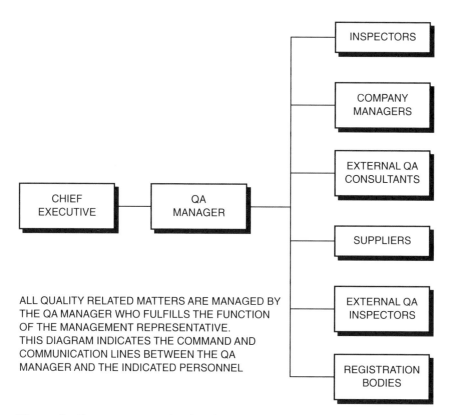

ALL QUALITY RELATED MATTERS ARE MANAGED BY
THE QA MANAGER WHO FULFILLS THE FUNCTION
OF THE MANAGEMENT REPRESENTATIVE.
THIS DIAGRAM INDICATES THE COMMAND AND
COMMUNICATION LINES BETWEEN THE QA
MANAGER AND THE INDICATED PERSONNEL

Figure 9: Company organisation for management of quality assurance

T. BEAR DESIGN & MANUFACTURING	ISSUE #: 1
PART 1: SECTION 1	ISSUE DATE: 1/12/9X
SUBJECT: MANAGEMENT RESPONSIBILITY	PAGE 6 OF 6

1.3 MANAGEMENT REVIEW

All elements of the QA manual are reviewed regularly to ensure that they are relevant and suitable for our business. The review schedule is decided upon by the QA manager and all elements are reviewed at least annually. All managers affected by a change in procedure are consulted in advance, for comment. The records of the reviews are in the possession of the QA manager.

RELEVANT PROCEDURES AND REFERENCE
Review of Quality Management System – QAP 1

T. BEAR DESIGN & MANUFACTURING	ISSUE #: 2
PART 1: SECTION 2	ISSUE DATE: 1/12/9X
SUBJECT: QUALITY SYSTEM	PAGE 1 OF 2

2.1 THE QUALITY ASSURANCE MANUAL

The function of this manual is to:

state our policy towards quality;

define our QA system;

document our methods in realising our quality policy;

act as the reference book for our staff in quality related matters;

demonstrate our compliance with ISO9001.

2.2 MANUAL CONTENTS

For convenience, the manual is in two functional parts.

Part 1 includes the company's policy towards each aspect of the ISO9001 standard and is arranged with reference to that standard.

The specific methods and resources used to carry out our work, referred to as work instructions and quality assurance procedures are contained in Part 2. The list of documents used in the quality management system, referred to as standard documents (SDs), and appendices to the manual are also in Part 2.

2.3 ISSUE AND AMENDMENT OF THE MANUAL

2.3.1 The manual is regularly reviewed as stated in Section 1.

T. BEAR DESIGN & MANUFACTURING	ISSUE #: 1
PART 1: SECTION 2	ISSUE DATE: 1/12/9X
SUBJECT: QUALITY SYSTEM	PAGE 2 OF 2

2.3.2 All issues/amendments are managed by the QA manager. For clarity, complete sections or individual procedures are issued. Thus, although only a paragraph may be revised, the complete section or procedure is reissued. Amendment record sheets are issued with the revised item and replace superseded record sheets.

2.3.3 The manual is issued only to staff on the distribution list. These staff are responsible for maintaining their copy of the manual. The manual may not be distributed to anybody else without the written authorisation of the QA manager.

2.4 SPECIFIC CONTRACT REQUIREMENTS

2.4.1 The general quality plan shown in Appendix 2 is to be used unless the customer specifically requests an alternative plan.

2.4.2 Any alternative plans are devised and approved by the QA manager and the customer.

2.4.3 In all cases, the level of quality of any plan must reach or exceed that of our general quality plan.

RELEVANT PROCEDURES AND REFERENCE
Document Control – Issue and Amendment – QAP 6

T. BEAR DESIGN & MANUFACTURING	ISSUE #: 1
PART 1: SECTION 3	ISSUE DATE: 1/12/9X
SUBJECT: CONTRACT REVIEW	PAGE 1 OF 1

3.1 All enquiries are checked to ensure enough information has been supplied to allow us to quote. The process of dealing with an enquiry is defined in a procedure.

3.2 Quotations must be approved by the chief estimator. The process of preparing quotations/estimates is defined in a procedure.

3.3 As orders are received, they are processed in accordance with a documented procedure prior to any design or manufacturing activity. All orders are confirmed with the customer prior to commencing design/manufacturing.

3.4 All contracts are initially reviewed by the senior managers within one week of receipt of the order. Thereafter, contracts are reviewed every week unless agreed otherwise at a review meeting.

3.5 Records of review meetings are maintained and stored in each relevant contract file.

RELEVANT PROCEDURES AND REFERENCE
Enquiries and Order Processing – QAP 2
Preparing Quotations – QAP 3

T. BEAR DESIGN & MANUFACTURING	ISSUE #: 1
PART 1: SECTION 4	ISSUE DATE: 1/12/9X
SUBJECT: DESIGN CONTROL	PAGE 1 OF 2

4.1 GENERAL

4.1.1 All work of the design department, including the preparation of drawings, models and calculations are controlled by procedures to ensure that the design requirements are met.

4.1.2 Relevant codes of practice, standards and technical data are maintained in a technical library.

4.2 DESIGN AND DEVELOPMENT PLANNING

4.2.1 All design drawings, models and calculations are referenced to the contract number.

4.2.2 The general quality plan is used to plan the design function. Should a contract require a specific plan, this can be produced, subject to our quality policy towards quality plans.

4.2.3 All staff are trained to carry out the work undertaken in the design department.

4.3 DESIGN INPUT

4.3.1 All contract documentation is checked, prior to commencing work, that it is complete and meets statutory legislation. Any conflict is advised to the customer and remedied, prior to starting design work. In all cases, statutory legislation must prevail.

4.3.2 All meetings where design discussions take place are noted and any relevant data placed in the contract file.

T. BEAR DESIGN & MANUFACTURING	ISSUE #: 1
PART 1: SECTION 4	ISSUE DATE: 1/12/9X
SUBJECT: DESIGN CONTROL	PAGE 2 OF 2

4.4 DESIGN OUTPUT

4.4.1 All drawings, models and calculations produced by the design department meet relevant standards, codes of practice and statutory legislation.

4.5 DESIGN VERIFICATION

4.5.1 Design approval is carried out by the design manager or trained staff nominated by the design manager.

4.5.2 Previous designs of a similar nature may be compared or other staff consulted where necessary.

4.6 DESIGN CHANGES

4.6.1 All changes are noted with the reasons for the changes. All changes must be approved internally and by the customer.

4.6.2 The issue of drawings and calculation sheets is subject to the document control procedures as specified in Section 5 of this manual – Part 1. Models are subject to the same procedures, and are referenced to the drawings and contract.

RELEVANT PROCEDURES AND REFERENCE
Contract Planning – QAP 4
Design Department – Control – QAP 5
Document Control – Issue and Amendment – QAP 6

T. BEAR DESIGN & MANUFACTURING	ISSUE #: 1
PART 1: SECTION 5	ISSUE DATE: 1/12/9X
SUBJECT: DOCUMENT CONTROL	PAGE 1 OF 1

5.1 DOCUMENT APPROVAL AND ISSUE

5.1.1 All documents essential to the contracts undertaken are approved and issued in accordance with procedures. These procedures ensure that the quality of the document contents is in accordance with industry practice.

5.1.2 Standards, codes of practice and statutory legislation are maintained and a log-book used to control their distribution.

5.1.3 Procedures are used to control documents including:

design output from the design department;

manufacturing input such as material lists.

5.1.4 All of these procedures ensure that:

documents are approved for issue to the relevant people;

each document is recognisable by an issue number and issue date;

documents are removed from circulation as soon as they are rendered obsolete.

5.2 DOCUMENT CHANGES/MODIFICATIONS

5.2.1 The procedures referred to in this section also ensure that changes/modifications are dealt with in a similar way to the initial document issue.

5.2.2 Changes/modifications are noted and distributed to the relevant people. These new issues are also recorded in the same way as the original issue.

RELEVANT PROCEDURES AND REFERENCE
Document Control – Issue and Amendment – QAP 6

T. BEAR DESIGN & MANUFACTURING	ISSUE #: 1
PART 1: SECTION 6	ISSUE DATE: 1/12/9X
SUBJECT: PURCHASING	PAGE 1 OF 2

6.1 GENERAL

The company operates procedures which ensure that all goods and services purchased meet our requirements.

6.2 ASSESSMENT OF SUB-CONTRACTORS

6.2.1 The company maintains list of approved suppliers. Where possible, goods/services are purchased only from approved suppliers. When we cannot purchase from an approved supplier, the QA manager is consulted and will recommend a course of action.

6.2.2 Suppliers are assessed with reference to their overall service. The criteria for assessment are updated on a regular basis by the QA manager, who will seek the advice of other managers.

The assessments may include:

visits to the supplier's site;

examination of samples;

use of formal questionnaires.

6.2.3 Our procedures also consider consistency of service by the supplier. An inconsistent or low standard of service may result in a supplier being de-listed from the approved suppliers list.

T. BEAR DESIGN & MANUFACTURING	ISSUE #: 1
PART 1: SECTION 6	ISSUE DATE: 1/12/9X
SUBJECT: PURCHASING	PAGE 2 OF 2

6.3 PURCHASING DATA

6.3.1 All purchase orders are placed by the buyers.
The purchase order must:
> be clear and unambiguous;
>
> refer to data sheets, standards and codes of practice where possible;
>
> request certificates of authenticity where required by the contract or statutory legislation.

Request our or our customer's representative to visit the supplier to verify the goods/services supplied.

6.4 VERIFICATION OF PURCHASED PRODUCT

6.4.1 All customers will be given reasonable access to visit our company or our suppliers to verify that purchased goods/ services meet the requirements of their contracts.

6.4.2 We recognise that a customer's verification of purchased product does not relieve us of our responsibilities towards quality.

RELEVANT PROCEDURES AND REFERENCE
Purchasing methods – QAP 7
Vendor Assessment and Supplier Approval – QAP 8

T. BEAR DESIGN & MANUFACTURING	ISSUE #: 1
PART 1: SECTION 7	ISSUE DATE: 1/12/9X
SUBJECT: PURCHASER SUPPLIED PRODUCT	PAGE 1 OF 1

7.1 Where purchaser supplied product is provided, it will be inspected upon receipt to ensure that it meets our requirements. Unless otherwise specified, it will undergo the same inspection and quality assurance procedures that are relevant to material purchased from our suppliers.

7.2 Specific procedures are in place to ensure that it is identified upon receipt and used in relevant contracts as per the customer's instructions.

RELEVANT PROCEDURES AND REFERENCE
Purchaser Supplied Product – QAP 9

T. BEAR DESIGN & MANUFACTURING	ISSUE #: 1
PART 1: SECTION 8	ISSUE DATE: 1/12/9X
SUBJECT: PRODUCT IDENTIFICATION AND TRACEABILITY	PAGE 1 OF 1

8.1 All raw materials are identified by a reference number or description as they are received in our goods inwards stores.

8.2 As materials are withdrawn from stock and processed into manufactured products they are identified by the use of tags or labels, containing their stock reference number and/or description.

8.3 Where stipulated by legislation or contract, the identification of materials up to and including the manufactured product is recorded to permit traceability.

8.4 Certificates of origin and supplier material certificates are retained when required by contract or legislation.

RELEVANT PROCEDURES AND REFERENCE
Stock Control – QAP 10
Labelling of Finished Product – WI 1

T. BEAR DESIGN & MANUFACTURING	ISSUE #: 1
PART 1: SECTION 9	ISSUE DATE: 1/12/9X
SUBJECT: PROCESS CONTROL	PAGE 1 OF 2

9.1 GENERAL

9.1.1 The production department operates a careful planning operation laid down in a procedure.

9.1.2 All production methods are defined in procedures and staff are trained accordingly. The production manager is responsible for ensuring that staff are suitably trained.

9.1.3 All staff are responsible for the quality of their output. Manufacturing samples of a high quality are maintained and available for all staff to examine.

9.1.4 The organisation of the production department and the procedures used within it ensure that all work is carried out under controlled conditions and that a safe production department is maintained.

9.2 SPECIAL PROCESSES

9.2.1 The company considers the stitching of external fabrics a 'special process'. Special care is taken to ensure that there is strict control over the quality of output.

9.2.2 On a regular basis, external professional advice is sought on this process and specialised testing carried out by external approved laboratories.

This specialised testing includes both X-ray testing (non-destructive methods) and tension testing (destructive methods).

T. BEAR DESIGN & MANUFACTURING	ISSUE #: 1
PART 1: SECTION 9	ISSUE DATE: 1/12/9X
SUBJECT: PROCESS CONTROL	PAGE 2 OF 2

The results and conclusions of these tests are recorded and integrated into future designs.

RELEVANT PROCEDURES AND REFERENCE
Contract Planning – QAP 4
Production Control – QAP 11
Operation of Foam Filling Machine – WI 2
Operation of Stitching and Sewing Machines – WI 3
Labelling of Finished Product – WI 1

T. BEAR DESIGN & MANUFACTURING	ISSUE #: 1
PART 1: SECTION 10	ISSUE DATE: 1/12/9X
SUBJECT: INSPECTION AND TESTING	PAGE 1 OF 3

10.1 RECEIVING INSPECTION AND TESTING

10.1.1 All materials purchased are inspected upon receipt and compared against our purchase order for verification. This includes the checking of requested documentation such as certificates of conformity.

10.1.2 Materials failing to meet our infection are returned to our suppliers and the QA manager notified.

10.1.3 Materials at goods inwards are classified and segregated into three areas:

awaiting inspection;

passed inspection;

rejected at inspection.

10.1.4 Material issued under positive recall procedures is clearly labelled and its details recorded.

10.2 IN-PROCESS INSPECTION AND TESTING

10.2.1 During the production process, checks are carried out to verify that material is meeting our requirements as specified by relevant specifications. Material rejected is set aside for scrapping or reprocessing as appropriate.

10.2.2 The inspection and testing is carried out by trained staff as nominated by the QA manager.

10.2.3 Should any material issued under positive recall procedures fail our inspection/testing, all the material of the batch issued is withdrawn and is completely examined.

T. BEAR DESIGN & MANUFACTURING	ISSUE #: 1
PART 1: SECTION 10	ISSUE DATE: 1/12/9X
SUBJECT: INSPECTION AND TESTING	PAGE 2 OF 3

10.2.4 Production planning and control has been organised to permit 'holding areas' for material that has not yet passed the relevant inspection and testing. These areas are clearly identified, as is all material in these areas.

10.3 FINAL INSPECTION AND TESTING

10.3.1 All finished products are examined both functionally and visually.

10.3.2 All inspection and test records generated in previous tests are verified. These records are reviewed daily by management to ensure that we are operating an effective quality system.

10.3.3 Contract requirements for particular inspection and testing are carried out where specified.

10.3.4 Any materials failing final inspection and testing are speedily removed and either reprocessed or scrapped as appropriate.

10.4 INSPECTION AND TEST RECORDS

10.4.1 Records generated during the inspection and test procedures are maintained as described in our QA manual – quality records section.

10.4.2 The following records are maintained to verify our control of inspection and test.

T. BEAR DESIGN & MANUFACTURING	ISSUE #: 1
PART 1: SECTION 10	ISSUE DATE: 1/12/9X
SUBJECT: INSPECTION AND TESTING	PAGE 3 OF 3

goods – inwards checklists and copy of purchase request;

in-process dimensional checklists;

material rejection reports;

final inspection and test certificates.

RELEVANT PROCEDURES AND REFERENCE
Incoming Material Inspection – QAP 12
Positive Recall Measures – QAP 14
Statistical Procedure – QAP 24
In-process Dimensional Checks – WI 5
Functional and Visual Checks of Completed Product – WI 6
Control of Reject Material – WI 7

T. BEAR DESIGN & MANUFACTURING	ISSUE #: 1
PART 1: SECTION 11	ISSUE DATE: 1/12/9X
SUBJECT: INSPECTION, MEASURING AND TEST EQUIPMENT	PAGE 1 OF 1

11.1 The company operates procedures to ensure that our design and production specifications are reviewed to identify suitable inspection, measuring and test equipment that may be used to check our conformance with the specifications.

11.2 The correct equipment is purchased, rented or loaned from relevant sources in order that conformance checks can take place.

11.3 Details of equipment are recorded including its name, serial number and description, together with its location. This ensures each piece of equipment is uniquely identifiable.

11.4 Procedures are used to calibrate accurately, all inspection measuring and test equipment on a systematic basis to specifications, which are traceable to international standards, where possible. These calibration procedures ensure that calibration is carried out systematically and that calibration adjustments are only carried out under control.

11.6 Where possible, calibration adjustment features are locked or made accessible only to calibration personnel.

11.7 All equipment is operated, handled and stored in accordance with manufacturer's instructions.

11.8 In the event that a piece of equipment is found to be out of calibration, previous records are assessed for validity and noted. The QA manager will decide on appropriate action to take, if the quality of our product is affected.

11.9 All calibration records are available to our customers, when stipulated in the contract.

RELEVANT PROCEDURES AND REFERENCE
Equipment Checks and Calibration – QAP 16

T. BEAR DESIGN & MANUFACTURING	ISSUE #: 1
PART 1: SECTION 12	ISSUE DATE: 1/12/9X
SUBJECT: INSPECTION AND TEST STATUS	PAGE 1 OF 1

12.1 All reject and scrap material is clearly identified and placed in suitable containers.

12.2 Throughout production all material can be clearly identified according to its test status, by the use of appropriate labelling or placement in a segregation area. The method of labelling will be determined by the QA and production managers, and made available to all relevant staff.

12.3 The inspection and test reports are checked prior to dispatch to ensure that all materials meet specification. Dispatch documents are only released after this final inspection.

12.4 The dispatch documents are signed by nominated personnel who will ensure that all previous inspection and test reports have been completed and signed by the correct authorities.

RELEVANT PROCEDURES AND REFERENCE
Placement and Material Identification – QAP 17
Labelling of Finished Product – WI 1

T. BEAR DESIGN & MANUFACTURING	ISSUE #: 1
PART 1: SECTION 13	ISSUE DATE: 1/12/9X
SUBJECT: CONTROL OF NONCONFORMING PRODUCT	PAGE 1 OF 1

13.01 The company operates procedures to ensure adequate control of all material that fails to meet our specifications. These procedures prevent such material being used or sent to our customers.

13.02 The procedures ensure that such material is identified, segregated, noted and disposed with in a consistent way.

13.1 NONCONFORMITY REVIEW AND DISPOSITION

13.1.1 The company's procedures ensure that nominated staff will review all actions taken regarding nonconforming material.

13.1.2 The review will address all relevant information and decide on a course of action which will determine if the material is:

1 reprocessed to meet our requirements; or

2 accepted for use with or without rework after permission has been received by the customer; or

3 used for an alternative purpose for which it is suitable; or

4 rejected completely and scrapped.

13.1.3 In all cases the material will be clearly identified and reinspected to meet our requirements, unless scrapped. The actions taken will be recorded and, where appropriate, the actions for rework etc. noted on instructions to relevant personnel.

RELEVANT PROCEDURES AND REFERENCE
Nonconforming Product – QAP 18

T. BEAR DESIGN & MANUFACTURING	ISSUE #: 1
PART 1: SECTION 14	ISSUE DATE: 1/12/9X
SUBJECT: CORRECTIVE ACTION	PAGE 1 OF 1

14.1 The company operates procedures that involve regular review of all records generated by our system, plus other records that the QA manager chooses. Any trends are investigated and appropriate remedial action taken.

14.2 All procedures are regularly reviewed with a view to improvement that will lower our risk of producing nonconforming material.

14.3 Management and other staff nominated by management attend these review meetings.

14.4 The corrective actions are also analysed for effectiveness and appropriate changes made to our method of analysis if required.

14.5 Where necessary, procedures are altered and recorded as a result of this corrective action.

14.6 All customer complaints are reviewed regularly and analysed to determine the causes of complaints. Remedial action is taken promptly to minimise the number of complaints.

RELEVANT PROCEDURES AND REFERENCE
Analysis of Quality System – QAP 20
Customer Complaints – QAP 25

T. BEAR DESIGN & MANUFACTURING	ISSUE #: 1
PART 1: SECTION 15	ISSUE DATE: 1/12/9X
SUBJECT: HANDLING, STORAGE, PACKAGING AND DELIVERY	PAGE 1 OF 2

15.1 GENERAL

The company operates procedures which ensure that all materials are protected from loss or damage during handling, storage, packaging and delivery to the customer.

15.2 HANDLING

All materials are handled in a manner that will prevent loss or damage. Through experience we have developed methods to ensure safe and careful movement of material within our company. Management in each department ensure that staff are adequately trained to move materials when required.

15.3 STORAGE

The company ensures that adequate storage facilities are made available for materials from receipt at goods inwards to their final dispatch to customers.

Materials are always identifiable and stored in the appropriate racks and containers.

Where necessary, the company will provide a controlled environment for materials as, for example, in the storage of flammable materials.

Relevant staff are trained in storage methods and periodic checks are carried out to ensure that our methods are both efficient and safe.

T. BEAR DESIGN & MANUFACTURING	ISSUE #: 1
PART 1: SECTION 15	ISSUE DATE: 1/12/9X
SUBJECT: HANDLING, STORAGE, PACKAGING AND DELIVERY	PAGE 2 OF 2

15.4 PACKAGING

Material is packaged with suitable material where necessary. The packaging is designed to prevent damage and to display identification marks/labels that are affixed to the materials.

Where a customer's special packaging requirements are stipulated in a contract, these shall be honoured and will not be of a lesser standard of quality than our usual packaging.

Relevant staff are trained to use packaging equipment in a safe manner.

15.5 DELIVERY

Dispatch documents clearly identifying the destination, customer, contract and product are forwarded with each consignment. Where necessary, these will include specific handling requirements.

RELEVANT PROCEDURES AND REFERENCE
Stock Control – QAP 10
Dispatch – QAP 19

T. BEAR DESIGN & MANUFACTURING	ISSUE #: 1
PART 1: SECTION 16	ISSUE DATE: 1/12/9X
SUBJECT: QUALITY RECORDS	PAGE 1 OF 2

16.1 The company maintains QA related records specified below which record the performance and achievements of our QA system.

16.2 The records are created by relevant personnel at the times required by our system.

16.3 Records are available to management staff and to staff nominated by the QA manager. For reasons of confidentiality, some historical records are of limited access and are restricted to the QA manager and others nominated by this manager.

16.4 The records are retained for the minimum time indicated on the attached table.

T. BEAR DESIGN & MANUFACTURING	ISSUE #: 1
PART 1: SECTION 16	ISSUE DATE: 1/12/9X
SUBJECT: QUALITY RECORDS	PAGE 2 OF 2

QUALITY RECORDS – MANAGEMENT SYSTEM			
RECORD TYPE	INDEXING METHOD	OFFICIAL HOLDER	RETENTION PERIOD
MANAGEMENT REVIEW REPORTS	DATE	QA MANAGER	5 YEARS
PURCHASE REQUESTS	NUMERICAL	BUYER	5 YEARS
APPROVED SUPPLIER LISTS	DATE	QA MANAGER	5 YEARS
CONTRACTS	NUMERICAL/ YEAR	SALES MANAGER	10 YEARS
VENDOR ASSESSMENT RECORDS	NUMERICAL/ DATE	QA MANAGER	10 YEARS
INSPECTION AND TEST RECORDS	NUMERICAL/ DATE	QA MANAGER	10 YEARS
TRACEABILITY RECORDS AND CERTIFICATES OF CONFORMITY	NUMERICAL/ DATE	QA MANAGER	5 YEARS
AUDIT REPORTS	NUMERICAL	QA MANAGER	10 YEARS

RELEVANT PROCEDURES AND REFERENCE
Document Control – Issue and Amendment – QAP 6

T. BEAR DESIGN & MANUFACTURING	ISSUE #: 1
PART 1: SECTION 17	ISSUE DATE: 1/12/9X
SUBJECT: INTERNAL QUALITY AUDITS	PAGE 1 OF 1

17.1 Internal quality audits are carried out to check that we are following procedures and to assess their effectiveness.

17.2 The QA manager designs an audit schedule to ensure that all quality related activities are audited at least annually.

17.3 The quality reports (SD15) are reviewed by the QA manager and the quality management review team, and appropriate corrective action taken.

17.4 Records of audits and relevant corrective action are maintained for a period of five years.

RELEVANT PROCEDURES AND REFERENCE
Quality System – Internal Audits – QAP 21

T. BEAR DESIGN & MANUFACTURING	ISSUE #: 1
PART 1: SECTION 18	ISSUE DATE: 1/12/9X
SUBJECT: TRAINING	PAGE 1 OF 1

18.1 The company operates procedures to ensure that all staff are trained to carry out work to meet our contract requirements.

18.2 Staff are selected based on their aptitude and ability to carry out their work.

18.3 All staff are encouraged to develop their skills, and adequate training courses and funds are made available.

18.4 The company maintains staff training records which are regularly reviewed and updated as appropriate. Any shortage of skills is noted and either new staff hired or existing staff trained.

| RELEVANT PROCEDURES AND REFERENCE |
| Training Procedures – QAP 22 |

T. BEAR DESIGN & MANUFACTURING	ISSUE #: 1
PART 1: SECTION 19	ISSUE DATE: 1/12/9X
SUBJECT: SERVICING	PAGE 1 OF 1

19.1 Defective products distributed to customers are replaced upon receipt of the complaint and proof of fault.

19.2 The company acts according to local safety legislation and will act promptly to meet our obligations in all cases of product defects or failure.

19.3 All repairs carried out in our factory are subject to the standard production test methods in force.

19.4 Repairs carried out under warranty are carried out subject to the conditions in the original customer contract.

RELEVANT PROCEDURES AND REFERENCE
Product Repair and Replacement Procedure – QAP 23

T. BEAR DESIGN & MANUFACTURING	ISSUE #: 1
PART 1: SECTION 20	ISSUE DATE: 1/12/9X
SUBJECT: STATISTICAL TECHNIQUES	PAGE 1 OF 1

20.1 The company operates statistical procedures in accordance with the terms of each customer contract. These sampling procedures are principally used at inspection of raw materials and prior to final dispatch.

20.2 In the absence of procedures being specified by the customer contract, the company operates to the general principle of the sampling techniques most commonly used in the customer's country. As an example, in the United Kingdom, the company operates methods based on BS6000 and 6001.

20.3 Records of all statistical procedures are maintained and forwarded to the customer where necessary.

20.4 It is the responsibility of the QA manager to ensure that the correct sampling procedures are used.

RELEVANT PROCEDURES AND REFERENCE
Statistical Procedure – QAP 24

QUALITY ASSURANCE MANUAL PART 2

QA procedures
Work instructions
Standard documents
Appendices

TABLE OF CONTENTS

QUALITY ASSURANCE PROCEDURED

ISSUE DATE: 1/12/9X   ISSUE #:1

TITLE	ISSUE DATE	ISSUE	PAGES	REF
Review of quality management system	1/12/9X	2	1	1
Equiries and order processing	1/12/9X	1	2	2
Preparing quotations	1/12/9X	1	1	3
Contract planning	1/12/9X	1	1	4
Design department – control	1/12/9X	2	2	5
Document control – issue and amendment	1/12/9X	1	3	6
Purchasing methods	1/12/9X	1	2	7
Vendor assessment and supplier approval	1/12/9X	1	2	8
Purchaser supplied product	1/12/9X	1	1	9
Stock control	1/12/9X	2	1	10
Production control	1/12/9X	1	1	11
Incoming material inspection	1/12/9X	1	1	12
Positive recall measures	1/12/9X	2	1	14
Equipment checks and calibration	1/12/9X	1	1	16
Placement and material identification	1/12/9X	1	1	17
Nonconforming product	1/12/9X	1	1	18
Dispatch	1/12/9X	1	1	19
Analyses of quality system	1/12/9X	1	1	20
Quality system – internal audits	1/12/9X	1	1	21
Training procedures	1/12/9X	1	1	22
Product repair and replacement procedure	1/12/9X	1	1	23
Statistical procedure	1/12/9X	1	1	24
Customer complaints	1/12/9X	1	1	25

T. BEAR DESIGN & MANUFACTURING	ISSUE #: 2
PART 2: QAP # 1	ISSUE DATE: 1/12/9X
TITLE: REVIEW OF QUALITY MANAGEMENT SYSTEM	PAGE 1 OF 1

PURPOSE

To ensure that the quality system as defined in the quality manual is effective and relevant to our business.

PROCEDURE

The QA manager reviews the complete manual and procedures at least annually.

A review board is chosen by the QA manager to assist in the reviewing task. This board will have at least one representative from each department.

The review board will have at their disposal all records generated by the QA system, including audit reports and customer complaints.

The QA system report (SD1) will be used to record conclusions reached at each review.

All changes to the manual and procedures must be agreed upon by the managers affected by the changes.

All changes must be authorised by the QA manager.

All QA system reports are maintained by the QA manager for a period of three years.

T. BEAR DESIGN & MANUFACTURING	ISSUE #: 1
PART 2: QAP # 2	ISSUE DATE: 1/12/9X
TITLE: ENQUIRIES AND ORDER PROCESSING	PAGE 1 OF 2

PURPOSE

To define the methods used to process customer enquiries and orders in accordance with the customer's requirements.

PROCEDURE

All enquiries are logged in a sales enquiry book by the sales manager.

A standard customer enquiry form (SD2) is completed by the sales manager upon receipt of the enquiry. Should any further data be required for quotation, the customer is informed and requested to supply this data.

The customer enquiry documents and SD2 are passed to the chief estimator for estimating purposes.

All production requirements (delivery dates etc.) are agreed with the production manager, prior to submitting any quotation.

The quotation is submitted referencing all data supplied by the customer. This will include our quotation reference number.

All enquiry and quotation data are retained in a unique sales enquiry file.

Upon receiving a customer order, it is initially checked against the associated quotation. Any differences are noted and the customer informed. The order is confirmed once all the differences are solved.

After an order is confirmed, it is logged in the customer sales book.

This book is reviewed on a weekly basis by the QA manager. All contracts received in the previous week, are then reviewed by the senior managers at a contract review meeting.

T. BEAR DESIGN & MANUFACTURING	ISSUE #: 1
PART 2: QAP # 2	ISSUE DATE: 1/12/9X
TITLE: ENQUIRIES AND ORDER PROCESSING	PAGE 2 OF 2

At the contract review meetings, the senior managers decide on the priority of orders and allot their resources accordingly. A progress/planning report form (SD3) is used at each meeting to chart the stage that each contract has reached. The same form can be used as a planning chart.

T. BEAR DESIGN & MANUFACTURING	ISSUE #: 1
PART 2: QAP # 3	ISSUE DATE: 1/12/9X
TITLE: PREPARING QUOTATIONS	PAGE 1 OF 1

PURPOSE

To control the preparation of quotations prepared in response to customer enquiries.

PROCEDURE

The chief estimator receives a copy of the customer enquiry form (SD2) and customer supplied documentation from the sales manager.

The chief estimator may nominate another member of staff to prepare and supply the quotation.

Where further detail is required, the estimator will contact the customer directly.

The production manager and design staff will be asked for advice where required by the estimator, particularly where special design and production methods are required.

Particular attention is paid to legal requirements of the contract. Any queries on legal matters are referred to the chief executive for a decision.

Standard price lists are prepared from time to time by the sales department. Where possible these are used in preparing quotations.

After preparing the quotation, the chief estimator will countersign all quotation documents prior to dispatch to the customer.

The estimator is responsible for maintaining copies of all documentation forwarded to our customers. These are stored in the order of the enquiry number on SD2.

T. BEAR DESIGN & MANUFACTURING	ISSUE #: 1
PART 2: QAP # 4	ISSUE DATE: 1/12/9X
TITLE: CONTRACT PLANNING	PAGE 1 OF 1

All enquiries worth more than 2.5 per cent of the company turnover are referred to the chief executive for approval prior to sending the quotation to the customer.

PURPOSE

To ensure that contracts are produced to meet contract delivery dates.

PROCEDURE

All contracts are broken into smaller elements of design, production and packaging. The individual stages of outline design, design approval etc. are then planned by staff in the relevant departments.

Planning forms (SD4) are prepared and checked by the senior members of each department.

Regular planning meetings are held between departments to ensure that targets are met. The progress/planning report form is used to summarise the detailed information from the planning forms.

Where necessary, extra resources are made available to expedite contracts. Notes are maintained of these meetings and copies are maintained in each relevant contract file.

Any delays are notified in writing to the client. Where there is a financial penalty for late delivery, the chief executive is informed.

Any delays caused by the customer are recorded and the customer notified in writing, indicating the reasons and length/cost of the delay.

T. BEAR DESIGN & MANUFACTURING	ISSUE #: 2
PART 2: QAP # 5	ISSUE DATE: 1/12/9X
TITLE: DESIGN DEPARTMENT – CONTROL	PAGE 1 OF 2

PURPOSE

To ensure that the design department produces output to meet contract specifications.

PROCEDURE

The individual stages of outline design, design approval etc. are planned by staff in the design department. The design manager checks each contract to ensure that all design criteria are addressed. The planning form (SD4) may be used to record progress of each stage.

Standards, codes of practice and technical literature are maintained by the design manager. These are made available to relevant staff. The manager will ensure that only correct data are applied to each design.

Design teams are nominated by the design manager to deal with each contract. The design team is responsible for maintaining the contract files in their possession. This will include the use of document control procedures.

The use of standards and codes of practice is noted on the relevant drawings, models etc.

Records are maintained of all design meetings with the client and stored in the contract file.

All output of the design department, such as drawings and calculations, are referenced by the contract number. A second reference will indicate clearly the number and revision of the drawing, calculation sheet etc.

Drawings and calculation sheets are filed in numerical contract order.

T. BEAR DESIGN & MANUFACTURING	ISSUE #: 2
PART 2: QAP # 5	ISSUE DATE: 1/12/9X
TITLE: DESIGN DEPARTMENT – CONTROL	PAGE 2 OF 2

All output is checked, prior to issue, by the senior member of the design team.
Only client approved design output is used for production purposes.

Material specification lists are prepared by the design department from the approved documents and models.

T. BEAR DESIGN & MANUFACTURING	ISSUE #: 1
PART 2: QAP # 6	ISSUE DATE: 1/12/9X
TITLE: DOCUMENT CONTROL – ISSUE AND AMENDMENT	PAGE 1 OF 3

PURPOSE

To control the issue and amendment of documentation within our quality system. For clarity, this QA procedure is sub-divided into sections relevant to specific types of documents.

PROCEDURE – TECHNICAL LIBRARY

All standards and codes of practice are maintained by the design manager. A list of these is maintained and updated as new revisions are available. Any member of staff must 'sign out' each standard etc. by completing the library book. The title and number of the standard must be entered together with the signature of the person requiring their use.

Every effort is made to maintain up-to-date supplier information. These brochures are sorted by supplier name and available to all design staff. A signature is not required to use these brochures.

PROCEDURE: DESIGN OUTPUT

Internally approved documents/models are issued to the customer using the completed issue form (SD6).

A copy of this issue form is retained in the contract file.

Details of all output are recorded in the design register (SD7). The design register will be updated by the senior member of each design team. Details include reference number, short description and current status.

The status will be one of the following:

T. BEAR DESIGN & MANUFACTURING	ISSUE #: 1
PART 2: QAP # 6	ISSUE DATE: 1/12/9X
TITLE: DOCUMENT CONTROL – ISSUE AND AMENDMENT	PAGE 2 OF 3

A – approved by client with no comment – proceed with manufacture;

B – approved by client with comments – proceed with manufacture subject to the comments;

C – rejected by client – redesign required;

W– withdrawn or contract cancelled – file closed.

Any amendments required by the client are introduced on a new drawing etc., and a copy of the updated item forwarded to the customer for information purposes only using form SD6. All obsolete output is destroyed under the instruction of the design manager.

PROCEDURE – MATERIAL SPECIFICATION LISTS

Material specification lists are only prepared from customer approved (status 'A' or 'B') design output. These are prepared by the design teams and issued on the material specification list (SD8).

PROCEDURE – QUALITY ASSURANCE MANUAL

Changes to the manual are made by the QA manager only. These are issued to nominated staff listed in the manual distribution list prepared at regular intervals by the QA manager.

All issues and amendments are distributed with amendment sheets (SD9).

Each element of the manual (QA procedures etc.) is identified by a unique number, issue number and issue date. New issues always replace existing issues.

T. BEAR DESIGN & MANUFACTURING	ISSUE #: 1
PART 2: QAP # 6	ISSUE DATE: 1/12/9X
TITLE: DOCUMENT CONTROL – ISSUE AND AMENDMENT	PAGE 3 OF 3

CUSTOMER PRODUCT/PROMOTIONAL INFORMATION

Product information is prepared at regular intervals under the instruction of the chief executive officer.

This information is intended for promotional purposes and is marked with an issue date. Unless specifically stated, the contents of photographs or diagrams may be altered without immediate notice to the public.

T. BEAR DESIGN & MANUFACTURING	ISSUE #: 1
PART 2: QAP # 7	ISSUE DATE: 1/12/9X
TITLE: PURCHASING METHODS	PAGE 1 OF 2

PURPOSE

To ensure that suitable materials and services are purchased to honour customer contracts.

PROCEDURE

The purchasing system works to the following steps.

1 Purchase request form (SD10) is completed by the storeman indicating:

at least one approved supplier's name, if known;

material description and quantity;

supplier's stock number, if known;

relevant drawings and contract(s) – or if for 'stock';

relevant standards, statutory specification;

certificates of origin/conformity;

packaging.

2 Purchase request form is approved for processing by production manager. Non-approved requests are discarded.

3 A buyer checks the purchase request form for accuracy and to ensure that it is completed correctly.

4 The buyer will contact suppliers including any listed on the purchase request form for their quotations. Purchases are made from approved suppliers where possible. The QA manager is consulted where other suppliers are required and will recommend a course of action.

T. BEAR DESIGN & MANUFACTURING	ISSUE #: 1
PART 2: QAP # 7	ISSUE DATE: 1/12/9X
TITLE: PURCHASING METHODS	PAGE 2 OF 2

5 The supplier meeting the requirements of the order and quoting the lowest price will be given the order. The purchase request form is signed by the buyer and any additional terms of contract noted on the purchase request form. Orders by telephone will be issued in writing within two working days.

6 Order acknowledgements from suppliers are checked against orders and any differences remedied.

7 The purchase request form has a number of copies, which are distributed as follows:

White – supplier
Blue – filed in numerical order (order no.) in buyer's department
Pink – storeman
Green – to contract files, if the order only refers to one contract.

8 The storeman is responsible for expediting orders and will keep purchase request forms in an 'open file' until the order is received. In addition, the storeman after ensuring deliveries are complete, will return the copy of the form to the relevant buyer. Any delivery notes and related documents will be attached. The pink form is then attached to the related blue form.

9 Any damages or late deliveries are noted by the storeman and the buyer notified. Remedial action will be taken by the buyer and the QA manager notified.

T. BEAR DESIGN & MANUFACTURING	ISSUE #: 1
PART 2: QAP # 8	ISSUE DATE: 1/12/9X
TITLE: VENDOR ASSESSMENT AND SUPPLIER APPROVAL	PAGE 1 OF 2

PURPOSE

To ensure suppliers are selected to provide materials and services that meet our specified requirements.

PROCEDURE

Suppliers are selected by the QA, production and finance managers. Selection criteria are agreed by these managers and reflect what we require of each type of supplier. Criteria are reviewed at least yearly to ensure that they are relevant and appropriate changes are made.

The vendor assessment form (SD11) is used to record supplier assessments. The sample of SD11 shows a completed form.

The company maintains two approved supplier lists:

'A' list – preferential suppliers
'B' list – used only when an 'A' supplier cannot meet an enquiry/ order.

POTENTIAL SUPPLIERS

Potential suppliers are assessed by a combination of:

the potential supplier completing supplier enquiry form (SD16);

visits to the supplier's site by the QA manager;

assessing samples of materials/service provided by the potential supplier;

advice from staff.

T. BEAR DESIGN & MANUFACTURING	ISSUE #: 1
PART 2: QAP # 8	ISSUE DATE: 1/12/9X
TITLE: VENDOR ASSESSMENT AND SUPPLIER APPROVAL	PAGE 2 OF 2

Potential suppliers achieving a rating of at least 60 per cent are placed on our 'B' list.

APPROVED SUPPLIERS

Approved suppliers are assessed at least yearly.

Those that achieve a rating of less than 40 per cent are removed from our approved supplier lists. They are then treated as a 'potential supplier' if they are assessed at a later date.

Those that achieve a rating of between 40 per cent and 70 per cent are placed on our 'B' list.

VENDOR ASSESSMENT DATA

All data are maintained and held by the QA manager. Approved supplier lists are distributed to holders of the QA manual.

These are distributed every three months, unless a supplier has been removed from the list.

This information is considered 'commercially sensitive' and may be disclosed only with the permission of the QA manager or chief executive.

T. BEAR DESIGN & MANUFACTURING	ISSUE #: 1
PART 2: QAP # 9	ISSUE DATE: 1/12/9X
TITLE: PURCHASER SUPPLIED PRODUCT	PAGE 1 OF 1

PURPOSE

To ensure purchaser supplied product is accepted and used to meet our quality levels and the customer's requirements.

PROCEDURE

All goods supplied by our customers for incorporation into their contracts with us are treated in the following manner:

1 The quantity and quality of the goods are checked on receipt, and an advice note is forwarded with these to our customer.

2 In the event of any discrepancy between our assessment of quantity/quality and the customer's delivery note, the customer is advised immediately. The QA manager is informed and will decide on the course of action.

3 The goods are labelled, identifying their contract reference number and the customer's name.

4 In the event of there being excess material supplied, the customer is informed by the QA manager and will either remove the excess or permit us to store the goods for later use with their future contracts with us.

5 The excess material will only be used in the customer's contracts and not in any other contract.

T. BEAR DESIGN & MANUFACTURING	ISSUE #: 2
PART 2: QAP # 10	ISSUE DATE: 1/12/9X
TITLE: STOCK CONTROL	PAGE 1 OF 1

PURPOSE

To ensure accurate control of materials used in contracts.

PROCEDURE

All materials are identified by suitable name tags etc. to allow easy management of stock.

The following system has been adopted to manage stock.

1 Incoming material is inspected against the relevant purchase request form (SD10). The volume/quantity of material is noted on the relevant stock card (SD12).

2 Material is issued to the production department upon receipt of a material specification list (SD8). The quantity of materials is deducted on the relevant stock card (SD12).

3 When the minimum stock level is reached as shown on the stock cards, purchase order forms are completed and processed. The minimum and maximum stock levels are set by the production manager.

4 Random checks are carried out by the QA manager to ensure that the correct stocks and records are maintained.

5 Material is managed on the FIFO (first in, first out) basis, unless the QA manager instructs otherwise.

T. BEAR DESIGN & MANUFACTURING	ISSUE #: 1
PART 2: QAP # 11	ISSUE DATE: 1/12/9X
TITLE: PRODUCTION CONTROL	PAGE 1 OF 1

PURPOSE

To ensure efficient control of the production department in meeting the customer's requirements.

PROCEDURE

At regular planning meetings, contracts are investigated and schedules agreed to meet the terms of the contracts. The planning form (SD4) is used by the production manager to plan the production schedule. Bar-charts or similar may also be used.

Customer approved drawings and material specification lists are issued to the production manager, together with any production related documentation in the contract.

These are checked for accuracy by the production manager. The drawings and material specification lists are then issued to production staff. Specification lists are given to the storeman who will then issue the specified materials.

In the event of material shortages, the production manager and QA manager are informed and will decide upon a course of action to fulfil the contract.

Any special processes are identified at an early stage and action taken to carry out these processes. These are normally under the direct control of the production manager. Where external testing companies are required, the QA manager assumes control.

Any delays are notified to the production manager, who will then allocate resources where available. In the event of a contract being delayed, the QA manager is informed as soon as the delay is apparent. The customer will be contacted and an agreement reached on an alternative delivery date. It is our company policy to meet delivery schedules.

T. BEAR DESIGN & MANUFACTURING	ISSUE #: 1
PART 2: QAP # 12	ISSUE DATE: 1/12/9X
TITLE: INCOMING MATERIAL INSPECTION	PAGE 1 OF 1

PURPOSE

To ensure materials purchased meet specified requirements.

PROCEDURE

Copies of approved purchase request forms (SD10) are retained in the stores until all materials are received or the order is cancelled.

All materials received are checked against the relevant purchase request. This includes checking any documentation requested. The quantity and quality of all items are checked. Where specified on our purchase request form, the storeman will use a sampling procedure.

Where material requires further inspection it is placed 'on hold'. The QA manager is informed and will organise the inspection process.

Rejected material will be labelled, and the buyer and QA manager informed. They will then decide on remedial action, which normally involves contacting the supplier of the material.

Shortages, late deliveries or damage are noted on the purchase order form. The buyer is immediately informed of these problems. The purchase request form is retained by the storeman until the order is complete. In the event of material shortages that immediately delay production, the production manager and QA manager are informed, and will decide upon a course of action.

Any supplier documentation signed for receipt of goods will indicate damage, late delivery or shortage where they occur.

Any materials requiring special handling will be labelled clearly by the storeman.

Materials that are accepted as 'fit for use' are entered into our stock system as described separately.

T. BEAR DESIGN & MANUFACTURING	ISSUE #: 2
PART 2: QAP # 14	ISSUE DATE: 1/12/9X
TITLE: POSITIVE RECALL MEASURES	PAGE 1 OF 1

PURPOSE

To ensure materials issued, without inspection from stores, are controlled and clearly identified.

PROCEDURE

Sometimes material is required urgently in the production department and the normal receiving inspection and testing is not carried out.

This material is entered as stock, clearly labelled as 'untested' and separated from other stock.

The material is processed separately and undergoes all other inspection and tests carried out in the production department.

If any material fails these tests, the complete batch is inspected. Rejected material is isolated and the cause of failure determined where possible. The production manager and QA manager will then decide whether to reject the full batch or process the material that has passed inspection.

The QA manager will arrange with the buyer for the supplier to be contacted and the materials replaced where appropriate.

T. BEAR DESIGN & MANUFACTURING	ISSUE #: 1
PART 2: QAP # 16	ISSUE DATE: 1/12/9X
TITLE: EQUIPMENT CHECKS AND CALIBRATION	PAGE 1 OF 1

PURPOSE

To ensure that inspection, measuring and test equipment is maintained and records maintained.

PROCEDURE

The list of equipment controlled under this procedure is maintained by the QA manager in a test equipment register. A sample page of the register is shown as SD14.

All equipment is maintained and used in accordance with the supplier's instructions. These instructions are available to operators of the equipment.

Calibrations are carried out by trained staff or external companies where necessary. Where possible, calibrations are carried out to international standards.

Calibration records are retained by the QA manager. These records are available to customers when requested.

The QA manager has set 'action limits' on each piece of test equipment. When equipment is found to be out of calibration and inside these limits, the equipment is calibrated. The 'action' limits are noted on the calibration notes for each machine.

If equipment is found to be outside these limits, the QA manager is informed immediately and will retest all products that have passed testing since the last calibration.

Where product safety has been affected the chief executive officer is consulted and products will be recalled from customers where necessary.

T. BEAR DESIGN & MANUFACTURING	ISSUE #: 1
PART 2: QAP # 17	ISSUE DATE: 1/12/9X
TITLE: PLACEMENT AND MATERIAL IDENTIFICATION	PAGE 1 OF 1

PURPOSE

To ensure that all materials at all stages of processing are correctly identifiable and in locations suitable for use.

PROCEDURE

In the company, all storage racks and containers for material are coloured to the following code:

Green – passed inspection

Orange – awaiting inspection

Red   – failed inspection.

All staff are obliged to follow this method of material storage.

All material, not on a workbench, and not stored according to the above method is to be placed in a red storage area. This will ensure that all production material passes inspection.

Unless stated on the purchase request form (SD10), all incoming material should be placed in a red storage area.

Material that has failed inspection must have a note attached, indicating the reasons for failure. This will aid management to decide on whether the material is reworked or scrapped.

In the event that material cannot be stored in a container/area due to shape or size, it is to be labelled with colour tags indicating the inspection status. These tags are to be signed by the inspection staff.

T. BEAR DESIGN & MANUFACTURING	ISSUE #: 1
PART 2: QAP # 18	ISSUE DATE: 1/12/9X
TITLE: NONCONFORMING PRODUCT	PAGE 1 OF 1

PURPOSE

To ensure that all occurrences of nonconforming product are investigated and remedied.

PROCEDURE

Details of all nonconformances are recorded on the nonconformance report (SD17). This is completed by production staff as soon as possible after the nonconformance is noticed.

The completed form is given, initially, to the production manager for comment and a course of action will be decided upon. This is noted on the report which is then given to the QA manager.

The QA manager is consulted immediately when a complete batch of material fails inspection. This ensures that alternative sources of supply can be found quickly if needed.

Every month, all nonconformance reports are reviewed and analysed by a team of production staff and the QA manager.

Remedial action is decided upon and acted on by relevant staff. The remedial action is closely monitored by the QA manager to ensure that it is both effective and economic.

T. BEAR DESIGN & MANUFACTURING	ISSUE #: 1
PART 2: QAP # 19	ISSUE DATE: 1/12/9X
TITLE: DISPATCH	PAGE 1 OF 1

PURPOSE

To ensure that all products are dispatched according to the customer's requirements.

PROCEDURE

After production of a contract has been completed the finance department issue a dispatch note (SD18) to the staff supervisor responsible for packaging and dispatch.

The dispatch note will be completed by the supervisor and the customer contacted to ensure that the product is dispatched or collected on time.

All transport is by our staff or approved external carriers.

Any special instructions regarding delivery must be confirmed by the supervisor with the customer.

The company copies of the dispatch note must be returned to the finance department within three working days of dispatch to ensure correct invoicing.

All customer queries regarding loss or incomplete delivery must be directed to the finance department.

All dispatch notes are retained on file in numerical order and a copy is retained in the relevant contract file.

T. BEAR DESIGN & MANUFACTURING	ISSUE #: 1
PART 2: QAP # 20	ISSUE DATE: 1/12/9X
TITLE: ANALYSES OF QUALITY SYSTEM	PAGE 1 OF 1

PURPOSE

To review and remedy weaknesses in our QA management system.

PROCEDURE

Separate from our QA management review meetings, staff meet at least monthly to discuss all occurrences of low quality performance.

All data that may indicate low quality performance are analysed including:

customer complaints;

price reductions given to customers;

scrap levels;

inspection reports.

A quality performance report (SD19) is completed at each meeting, and this is copied to all management and staff notice boards.

Where possible, remedial action is taken immediately, by agreement with the QA manager.

Where low quality performance is caused by poor equipment, the company will take action to use alternative equipment as quickly as possible. This may involve the use of external approved suppliers on a sub-contract basis.

T. BEAR DESIGN & MANUFACTURING	ISSUE #: 1
PART 2: QAP # 21	ISSUE DATE: 1/12/9X
TITLE: QUALITY SYSTEM – INTERNAL AUDITS	PAGE 1 OF 1

PURPOSE

To check that the procedures and policies described in our QA manual are operated correctly.

PROCEDURE

A detailed audit schedule (SD22) is prepared and updated by the QA manager regularly, defining the timing and description of the items to be audited.

All procedures and instructions are reviewed at least annually. Where previous audits have noted problems the item will be reviewed at least every three months until two sequential audits give positive results.

Staff are selected by the QA manager to carry out the audits, based upon information from their training records.

The QA manager will carry out spot-checks to ensure that correct methods are used and that the auditor is able to carry out the task.

The auditors complete quality reports (SD15) during each audit. These are retained by the QA manager and copied to the production manager.

Meetings are held with the auditors and QA manager at least monthly to review the results of the audits. Corrective action will be decided upon at these meetings and carried out promptly.

All audit reports, including audit schedules and quality reports, are retained by the QA manager.

T. BEAR DESIGN & MANUFACTURING	ISSUE #: 1
PART 2: QAP # 22	ISSUE DATE: 1/12/9X
TITLE: TRAINING PROCEDURES	PAGE 1 OF 1

PURPOSE

To ensure that staff are suitably trained to carry out their work.

PROCEDURE

Staff training needs are decided upon at regular meetings between management and staff. The QA manager will decide the type and amount of training required, and make the necessary arrangements.

Where external training is required, only approved suppliers will be used. These are monitored using our normal vendor assessment procedures.

The QA manager regularly updates the training records (SD20) for all staff. These records are retained for a period of one year after employees leave the company and are then destroyed.

It is the responsibility of the QA manager to ensure that the company meets the requirements of legislation regarding data protection and confidentiality.

The job descriptions of staff are contained in the appendices and are updated yearly.

Where contracts require particular skills not available in the company, staff may be trained or external approved suppliers used.

A staff training matrix (SD24) is completed every three months for all staff and distributed to all managers.

T. BEAR DESIGN & MANUFACTURING	ISSUE #: 1
PART 2: QAP # 23	ISSUE DATE: 1/12/9X
TITLE: PRODUCT REPAIR AND REPLACEMENT PROCEDURE	PAGE 1 OF 1

PURPOSE

To define the methods used to organise repair and replacement of faulty products.

PROCEDURE

PRODUCT UNDER WARRANTY

On receipt of the product, its part number is checked on our computer system to ensure that the warranty is valid.

If the product is out of warranty, the customer is informed by the finance department of the costs to repair or replace the faulty item, and a purchase order is then required from the client. The product is then treated as a product 'out of warranty' as described below.

If the product is in warranty, the repair supervisor will complete a warranty form (SD21).

After completing the repairs or replacing the item if more cost-effective, the warranty claim is copied to both the QA manager and production manager. These are used in separate procedures to analyse our methods of operation.

PRODUCTS OUT OF WARRANTY

The product is repaired or replaced according to the customer's wishes and at their cost. All repair/replacement instructions are treated in the same way as a customer contract.

The applicable inspection and test procedures will be carried out and the item dispatched in the usual way.

T. BEAR DESIGN & MANUFACTURING	ISSUE #: 1
PART 2: QAP # 24	ISSUE DATE: 1/12/9X
TITLE: STATISTICAL PROCEDURE	PAGE 1 OF 1

PURPOSE

To define our standard methods of using statistical techniques.

PROCEDURE

This statistical procedure is used in the absence of any specific instructions in the customer contract. If alternative techniques are specified they must be agreed, in advance of use, by the QA manager.

The company uses both BS6000 and BS6001 sampling techniques to inspect material at all stages of production. These are retained by the QA manager and inspection staff are trained in their use.

Acceptance and rejection levels, as defined in these standards, must be followed at all times.

The QA manager will carry out random checks on staff to ensure that the standards are used correctly and has the final decision on the use of these standards.

T. BEAR DESIGN & MANUFACTURING	ISSUE #: 1
PART 2: QAP # 25	ISSUE DATE: 1/12/9X
TITLE: CUSTOMER COMPLAINTS	PAGE 1 OF 1

PURPOSE

To define methods in dealing with customer complaints.

PROCEDURE

Customer complaints are treated in the following sequence.

1 The member of staff receiving the complaint will complete a customer complaint form (SD23).

2 This is immediately copied to the sales manager, production manager and QA manager. These three managers will then decide on a course of action to answer the complaint.

3 The chief executive is briefed at weekly management meetings on the state of current complaints.

4 After the complaint has been actioned inside the company, the customer will be contacted and reasonable effort made to remedy any future problems.

5 At monthly staff meetings, staff are informed of the complaints and agreed solutions actioned by the relevant staff to prevent the complaint recurring.

6 The QA manager will note all actions regarding complaints on their copy of the complaint form. This is then distributed to relevant staff to update them.

TABLE OF CONTENTS

WORK INSTRUCTIONS

ISSUE DATE: 1/12/9X   ISSUE #:1

TITLE	ISSUE DATE	ISSUE	PAGES	REF
Labelling of finished product	1/12/9X	1	1	1
The remaining instructions referred to in our manual are not included as they are very specific to companies and would be of little use to the reader. *Normal practice would be to include in this section all the work methods used in the manufacturing, installation and inspection functions.* *These do not necessarily have to be cross-referenced to the other sections of the manual.*	***	*	*	*

T. BEAR DESIGN & MANUFACTURING	ISSUE #: 1
PART 2: WI # 1	ISSUE DATE: 1/12/9X
TITLE: LABELLING OF FINISHED PRODUCT	PAGE 1 OF 1

All products manufactured are fitted with a permanent label sewn to the outer fabric.

Instructions

All labels state the company name and the country of manufacture.

The labels are to be fitted as near as possible to the underside of each toy and all printed data on the label must be clearly legible.

The following instructions affect specific types of label or customer requirements.

Christmas Toys

Use label type 'CH – A' with the large blank section on outer side. Use the Tylen No. 3 machines to feed the labels.

Summer Range for American Customers

Affix standard label and the American safety tag – Ref. USA 345.

This tag must use identical information to that on the external packaging. The machining operator is to ensure that each external name tag matches the colour of the smaller safety tag. To demonstrate that this has been checked, the same operator must initial the 'QA Mark Number 1' before sending product to final inspection.

Large Easter Toys for European Markets

Use 'Euro-Tag' and sew to centre underside of toys. No other label must be fixed within 2 cm from either side of this label.

TABLE OF CONTENTS

STANDARD DOCUMENTS

ISSUE DATE: 1/12/9X   ISSUE DATE #:1

TITLE	ISSUE DATE	ISSUE	REF
QA system report	1/12/9X	1	1
Customer enquiry form	1/12/9X	1	2
Progress/planning report	1/12/9X	1	3
Planning form	1/12/9X	1	4
Issue form	1/12/9X	1	6
Design register	1/12/9X	1	7
Material specification list	1/12/9X	1	8
Amendment sheet	1/12/9X	1	9
Purchase request form	1/12/9X	1	10
Vendor assessment form	1/12/9X	1	11
Vendor assessment form (completed sample)	1/12/9X	1	11
Stock card	1/12/9X	1	12
Test equipment register	1/12/9X	1	14
Quality report	1/12/9X	1	15
Supplier enquiry form	1/12/9X	1	16
Nonconformance report	1/12/9X	1	17
Dispatch note	1/12/9X	1	18
Quality performance report	1/12/9X	1	19
Staff training record	1/12/9X	2	20
Warranty form	1/12/9X	1	21
Audit schedule	1/12/9X	1	22
Customer complaint form	1/12/9X	1	23
Staff training matrix	1/12/9X	2	24

T. Bear Design & Manufacturing	QA SYSTEM REPORT
	DOCUMENT REF.: SD1
	ISSUE #: 1
	ISSUE DATE: 1/12/9X

REVIEW DATE: / /	QA MANUAL REF:

SECTION/PROCEDURE ANALYSIS
ALL ITEMS MUST BE ANSWERED

ATTRIBUTE	Y/N	COMMENT
CONFORMS TO ISO9001		
RELEVANT TO BUSINESS		
CLEAR AND UNAMBIGUOUS		
REQUIRES REVISION		
TOO RESTRICTIVE TO USE		

GENERAL COMMENTS:

CORRECTIVE ACTION RECOMMENDED:

SIGNED:

T. Bear
Design & Manufacturing

CUSTOMER ENQUIRY FORM

DOCUMENT REF.: SD2

ISSUE #: 1

ISSUE DATE: 1/12/9X

DATE: / /

ENQUIRY #:

RECEIVED BY:

DATE: / /

EXISTING CUSTOMER: YES / NO

A/C NO IF KNOWN:

COMPANY NAME:

CONTACT:

PHONE:

ADDRESS:

FAX:

PRODUCTS REQUIRED:

REPLY BY: / /

DATA SUPPLIED BY CUSTOMER:

COMMENTS:

SIGNED:

		PROGRESS/PLANNING REPORT
T. Bear Design & Manufacturing		DOCUMENT REF.: SD3
		ISSUE #: 1
		ISSUE DATE: 1/12/9X

DATE: /   /

SHEET #:

THE EXPECTED COMPLETION DATE OF EACH STAGE IS TO BE ENTERED FOR EACH CONTRACT.
LATE CONTRACTS TO BE MARKED IN RED

CONTRACT REF #	DELIVERY DATE PROMISED	STAGE		
		DESIGN	MANUFACTURING	PACKAGING

SIGNED:

T. Bear Design & Manufacturing	**PLANNING FORM**
	DOCUMENT REF.: SD4
	ISSUE #: 1
	ISSUE DATE: 1/12/9X

DATE: / /	THE EXPECTED COMPLETION DATE OF EACH STAGE IS TO BE ENTERED.
CONTRACT REF.:	LATE CONTRACTS TO BE MARKED IN RED. DUE DATE IS DATE REQUIRED BY CONTRACT

STAGE OF WORK (OUTLINE DESIGN, APPROVAL ETC.)	DEPARTMENT:		
	COMPLETION DATE	DUE DATE	COMMENTS
COMPLETION			
SIGNED:			

T. Bear
Design & Manufacturing

ISSUE FORM

DOCUMENT REF.: SD6

ISSUE #: 1

ISSUE DATE: 1/12/9X

DATE: / /

ISSUED TO:

CONTRACT REF.:

DRAWING/MODEL DESCRIPTION	REF NO.	REV NO.	COMMENTS

SIGNED:

T. Bear **Design &** **Manufacturing**	**DESIGN REGISTER**							
	DOCUMENT REF.: SD7							
	ISSUE #: 1							
	ISSUE DATE: 1/12/9X							
CONTRACT REF.:	ANY OBSOLETE MATERIAL MUST BE INDICATED IN RED							
DRAWING/MODEL DESCRIPTION	REF NO.	REVISION NUMBER						
DESIGN TEAM NAME:								

T. Bear

Design &
Manufacturing

	MATERIAL SPECIFICATION LIST
	DOCUMENT REF.: SD8
	ISSUE #: 1
	ISSUE DATE: 1/12/9X

CONTRACT REF.:	PAGE # OF (must be completed)	
STOCK NUMBER	NAME	QUANTITY

SPECIAL PROCESSES/CONTRACT REQUIREMENTS

DESIGN TEAM NAME:

T. Bear

Design &
Manufacturing

AMENDMENT SHEET
DOCUMENT REF.: SD9
ISSUE #: 1
ISSUE DATE: 1/12/9X

ALL NEW AMENDMENTS REPLACE PRESENT DOCUMENTS.
REMOVE AND DESTROY OLD ISSUES

AMENDMENT	SECTION	PAGES	ISSUE DATE	ISSUE NUMBER

SIGNED:

T. Bear
Design & Manufacturing

PURCHASE REQUEST FORM
DOCUMENT REF.: SD10
ISSUE #: 1
ISSUE DATE: 1/12/9X

white – customer	blue – contract file
pink – invoicing	green – file in numerical order

SUPPLIER:	ORDER NO.:
	DATE: / /

ITEM	DESCRIPTION	SUPPLIER'S REFERENCE	QUANTITY	UNIT PRICE	TOTAL PRICE
			TOTAL PRICE		

SPECIAL INSTRUCTIONS:

SIGNED BY STOREMAN:

SIGNED BY MANAGER:

SIGNED BY BUYER:

VENDOR ASSESSMENT FORM

T. Bear

Design & Manufacturing

DOCUMENT REF.: SD11

ISSUE #: 1

ISSUE DATE: 1/12/9X

FOR INTERNAL USE ONLY – CONFIDENTIAL

SUPPLIER:		SUPPLIER NO.:
		DATE: / /

ITEM	CRITERIA	COMMENT	MAX RATING	RATING
		TOTALS		

COMMENTS:

RECOMMENDATION:

SIGNED:

VENDOR ASSESSMENT FORM
T. Bear Design & Manufacturing	DOCUMENT REF.: SD11

	DOCUMENT REF.: SD11
	ISSUE #: 1
	ISSUE DATE: 1/12/9X

FOR INTERNAL USE ONLY – CONFIDENTIAL

SUPPLIER: CLOTH SUPPLIER INC. MAIN STREET LONDON	SUPPLIER NO.: 123
	DATE: 14/12/9X

ITEM	CRITERIA	COMMENT	MAX RATING	RATING
1	QA SYSTEM	TO ISO9002	20	18
2	ENQUIRY RESPONSE TIME	NONE	15	12
3	DELIVERIES	IMPROVING	20	15
4	PRICING	PRICES LOWER IN NEW YEAR	20	10
5	PACKAGING	IS INSTALLING NEW MACHINERY	15	7
6	TECHNICAL DATA	AVERAGE	10	5
		TOTALS	100	67

COMMENTS:

APPEARS TO BE INVESTING IN A LOT OF NEW MACHINERY. QA SYSTEM IS IN OPERATION FOR 18 MONTHS AND IS VERY BENEFICIAL TO US

RECOMMENDATION:

MOVE TO 'A' LIST. REASSESS WITHIN A YEAR

SIGNED:

T. Bear

Design &
Manufacturing

STOCK CARD
DOCUMENT REF.: SD12
ISSUE #: 1
ISSUE DATE: 1/12/9X

MAXIMUM STOCK LEVEL: MINIMUM STOCK LEVEL:

MATERIAL DESCRIPTION:	STOCK NO.:
	CARD NO.:

DATE	IN	OUT	STOCK LEVEL

T. Bear Design & Manufacturing	TEST EQUIPMENT REGISTER
	DOCUMENT REF.: SD14
	ISSUE #: 1
	ISSUE DATE: 1/12/9X

INSPECTION, MEASURING AND TEST EQUIPMENT
CALIBRATION RECORDS MUST BE MAINTAINED ON ALL EQUIPMENT AND COMMENCE WHEN PURCHASED/RENTED

DESCRIPTION AND PURCHASE DATE	SERIAL NUMER	LOCATION

| QUALITY REPORT |
| DOCUMENT REF.: SD15 |
| ISSUE #: 1 |
| ISSUE DATE: 1/12/9X |

AUDIT DATE: / /   QA SECTION REF:

SECTION/PROCEDURE ANALYSIS

ITEMS UNDER AUDIT	QAP/WI #	COMMENT

CORRECTIVE ACTION RECOMMENDED:

SIGNED:

CORRECTIVE ACTION VERIFIED:

SIGNED:

QA MANAGER COMMENTS:

SIGNED:

	T. Bear Design & Manufacturing	**SUPPLIER ENQUIRY FORM**
		DOCUMENT REF.: SD16
		ISSUE #: 1
		ISSUE DATE: 1/12/9X

DATE: / /   ENQUIRY #:

RECEIVED BY: DATE: / /

EXISTING SUPPLIER: YES/NO ---- a/c no. if known:

COMPANY NAME:

CONTACT: PHONE:

ADDRESS: FAX:

PRODUCTS SUPPLIED:

QUALITY SYSTEM IN OPERATION: YES/NO

REGISTERED TO ISO STANDARD: YES/NO

   IF YES, STATE REGISTRATION NUMBER:

   IF NO, PLEASE DETAIL ON SEPARATE SHEETS YOUR EXISTING
   QUALITY ASSURANCE PROCEDURES AND CONTROL MEASURES

PLEASE GIVE TWO INDUSTRY REFERENCES THAT MAY BE
CONTACTED:

1

2

SIGNED:

T. Bear Design & Manufacturing	**NONCONFORMANCE REPORT**
	DOCUMENT REF.: SD17
	ISSUE #: 1
	ISSUE DATE: 1/12/9X

DATE: / /	REPORT #:

LOCATION OF PRODUCT:

BRIEF DESCRIPTION OF NONCONFORMANCE:

SIGNED:

SUPPLIER IF KNOWN:

COMMENTS: PRODUCTION MANAGER

SIGNED:	DATE: / /

COMMENTS: QA MANAGER

SIGNED:	DATE: / /

REVIEW MEETING COMMENTS

SIGNED:	DATE: / /

T. Bear

Design &
Manufacturing

DISPATCH NOTE
DOCUMENT REF.: SD18
ISSUE #: 1
ISSUE DATE: 1/12/9X

white – customer	blue – contract file
pink – invoicing	green – file in numerical order

CUSTOMER:

ORDER NO.:

DELIVERY DATE: /   /

ITEM	DESCRIPTION	OUR REFERENCE	QUANTITY	UNIT PRICE	TOTAL PRICE
				TOTAL PRICE	

SPECIAL INSTRUCTIONS:

SIGNED BY CUSTOMER:

SIGNED BY DISPATCH SUPERVISOR:

SIGNED BY DRIVER:

T. Bear

Design &
Manufacturing

QUALITY PERFORMANCE REPORT
DOCUMENT REF.: SD19
ISSUE #: 1
ISSUE DATE: 1/12/9X

REPORT NUMBER.:	ENTER NEW CRITERIA IN THE BLANK SECTIONS						
DESCRIPTION	LAST SIX MONTHS	NUMBER PER MONTH					
CUSTOMER COMPLAINTS							
FINISHED PRODUCT REJECTED INTERNALLY							
REDUCTIONS IN PRICE OFFERED TO CUSTOMERS							
DAMAGED GOODS RETURNED							

COMMENTS:

SIGNED:

		STAFF TRAINING RECORD	
	T. Bear Design & Manufacturing	DOCUMENT REF.: SD20	
		NAME:	
		EMPLOYEE #:	
		ISSUE DATE: 1/12/9X	ISSUE: 2

ABILITY	TASK
SUPERVISED	
UNSUPERVISED	
AUDIT	
COURSES	
NOTES	

RECORD SHEET NUMBER:	START DATE: / /

T. Bear

Design &
Manufacturing

WARRANTY FORM
DOCUMENT REF.: SD21
ISSUE #: 1
ISSUE DATE: 1/12/9X

DATE: / /   CUSTOMER REF:

RECEIVED BY: DATE: / /

WARRANTY EXPIRY DATE:

COMPANY NAME:

CONTACT: PHONE:

ADDRESS: FAX:

PRODUCTS REPORTED FAULTY:
PLEASE ENTER PART NUMBER AND DESCRIPTION OF FAULT

PRODUCTS:

REPAIR/REPLACE (circle the action taken)

SOURCE OF FAULT:

SIGNED: DATE: / /

T. Bear	AUDIT SCHEDULE
Design & Manufacturing	DOCUMENT REF.: SD22
	ISSUE #: 1
	ISSUE DATE: 1/12/9X

REPORT NUMBER.:	WHERE A NONCOMPLIANCE WAS NOTED, THE NEXT AUDIT WILL BE A MAXIMUM OF THREE MONTHS FROM THE LAST AUDIT
START DATE: / /	

QA SECTION NAME	REF #	NEXT AUDIT DUE:					

NOTES:

SIGNED:

T. Bear Design & Manufacturing	**CUSTOMER COMPLAINT FORM**
	DOCUMENT REF.: SD23
	ISSUE #: 1
	ISSUE DATE: 1/12/9X

DATE: / /

CUSTOMER NAME:

ADDRESS:

PHONE:

FAX:

FORM OF COMPLAINT	
RECEIVED BY	
NATURE OF COMPLAINT	
PRODUCTS MENTIONED	
REPLY REQUIRED	
TARGET DATE TO RESOLVE	
ACTION	
RESOLVED	
REVIEWED	
STATUS	ACTIONED RESOLVED REVIEWED

T. Bear **Design &** **Manufacturing**	**STAFF TRAINING MATRIX**				
	DOCUMENT REF.: SD24				
	ISSUE DATE: 1/12/9X		ISSUE #: 2		
	TASKS – REFER TO QAP/WI WHERE POSSIBLE S = CAN WORK UNDER SUPERVISION U = CAN WORK UNSUPERVISED				
STAFF NAMES					

APPENDICES

TABLE OF CONTENTS

APPENDICES TO MANUAL

ISSUE DATE: 1/12/9X   ISSUE #:1

TITLE	ISSUE DATE	ISSUE	PAGES	REF
Job descriptions	1/12/9X	2	1	1
General quality plan	1/12/9X	1	1	1
Company brochures are often included in this section	***	*	*	*

T. BEAR DESIGN & MANUFACTURING	ISSUE #: 2
APPENDICES NO.: 1	ISSUE DATE: 1/12/9X
SUBJECT: JOB DESCRIPTIONS	PAGE 1 OF 1

FOR REASONS OF CONFIDENTIALITY, ONLY THE QUALITY
ASSURANCE FUNCTION AND TASKS OF JOBS ARE DESCRIBED.

JOB TITLE	RESPONSIBILITIES AND TASKS
CHIEF EXECUTIVE OFFICER	manages the QA manager; attends regular management meetings where the QA system is reviewed; acts as final arbiter in legal issues relating to QA
QA MANAGER	carries out function of the QA management representative; management of all QA related matters; carries out vendor assessments; approves all vendor assessment reports; maintains and controls distribution of all QA related documentation
PRODUCTION MANAGER	ensures all production staff comply with the QA system; attends all QA review and contract review meetings; maintains training records; carries out vendor assessments and visits with chief buyer
DESIGN MANAGER	ensures all production staff comply with the QA system; maintains technical library; maintains contract files; approves all contract specifications prior to manufacture
CHIEF BUYER	carries out vendor assessments with production manager; maintains vendor assessments records; approves all purchase orders
etc.	etc.

T. BEAR DESIGN & MANUFACTURING	ISSUE #: 1
APPENDICES NO.: 2	ISSUE DATE: 1/12/9X
SUBJECT: GENERAL QUALITY PLAN	PAGE 1 OF 1

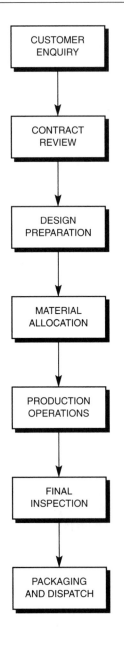

CUSTOMER ENQUIRY

Check order to ensure that an accurate estimate can be prepared. Seek further details where required. Confirm that we have the resources to design and manufacture to the enquiry. Prepare and supply estimate.

CONTRACT REVIEW

Check order against quotation for any differences. Clarify any with customer. Confirm order with customer. Plan design and manufacture.

DESIGN PREPARATION

Prepare design and approve internally. Secure customer approval. Prepare material specification list.

MATERIAL ALLOCATION

Purchase material if not in stock. Identify and allot materials for contract using material specification list. All material to be checked for compliance with specification

PRODUCTION OPERATIONS

Manufacture contact items with specified material. In-process inspection used to ensure compliance with specification.

FINAL INSPECTION

Final inspection and test carried out according to contract requirements. Statutory safety checks carried out.

PACKAGING AND DISPATCH

Packaging to contract specifications. Inspection of packaged items. All inspection documents are checked for accuracy. Dispatch note issued and goods dispatched according to contract.

APPENDIX I

Implementation of a QA system

As you will have seen from this book, a QA system designed around BS5750/ISO9000 addresses quality through management of the different business functions directly affecting your output, whether a product or service. From the initial customer enquiry, right through the design and production stages and finally the delivery and installation areas, we must investigate each QA function and define our aims and methods to manage quality.

For an effective management system rather than just a collection of separate schemes we now address how to integrate these into a cohesive QA system. In my own experience in attempting to introduce a system, deciding where to start is probably the hardest decision to make. All the QA functions affect each other and few companies have the time or money to allow the introduction of the QA system to adversely risk production or customer goodwill. This obviously places great pressure on the person implementing the system – the management representative – to be effective but not disruptive.

This book concentrates on a modular approach and by adapting the following implementation plan to your particular needs, some pain should be spared in designing and implementing the system. The methods described are based on my own experience and are not themselves part of the requirements of the standards. Therefore, if you disagree or see a better way to introduce the system, feel free to do so. I have assumed that the person introducing the system is the 'management representative' and has the responsibility and authority to introduce and manage the system.

If this person has not already been selected, then this must be the first step. In many small businesses this will be the general manager. Although it is preferred that the role of management representative is separate from other tasks, in many businesses it is economical that the role is shared with other responsibilities. The principal practical reason to separate the management representative is to ensure that their advice is impartial and that their decisions are not prejudiced towards any particular department in the business. For this reason many small businesses will have the general manager as the acting management representative and an assistant delegated to carry out some of the QA tasks such as maintenance of the QA manual.

The next step is to inform all staff that the company intends to introduce a QA system and expects all staff to participate in its success. As a rule, do not simply communicate this by a memorandum on the staff notice board. The implementation of the QA system is a step forward for a company, as important as the introduction of a new product. Therefore ensure that all employees are addressed either individually or in groups. Participation is the key to success of the system and ensuring that employees are part of the system and its success is essential. This emphasis on 'taking part' will obviously have to carry the backing of senior management. We are all reluctant to change our ways and without effective staff participation, attempting to introduce any system will fail. It is crucial to link the introduction of the system with improved customer satisfaction as this is our principal aim. Many employees incorrectly think that introduction of a QA system will improve efficiency at the cost of their jobs. Removing this barrier at the start is extremely important. Finally, do not associate the implementation of the QA system with any other company announcements. This simply reduces the initial impact of 'taking part' in the system that you want to nurture within employees. Similarly, do not link staff bonuses to the introduction of the system – if implementation does not go according to plan you will simply end up with some very unhappy employees!

Before introducing any changes, visit some companies, preferably in your industry sector, that already have systems, either partially or fully introduced. Like any other group of business people, a certain 'camaraderie' exists between QA managers and information gained at this early stage can help avoid many of the pitfalls as well as significantly reducing costs of implementation.

After you have gained some of the background knowledge, the next step is to address the standards in detail. This invariably necessitates becoming familiar with the different sections of the chosen

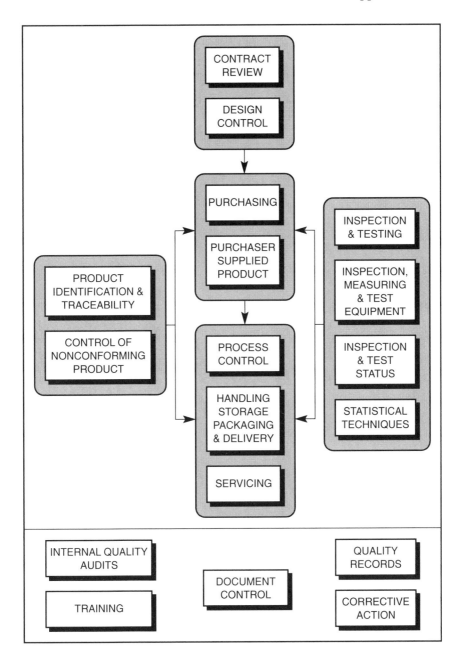

Figure A.1 Interaction of elements of a QA systems

ISO9000 standard that you wish to use. The interaction of the elements of an ISO 9001 QA system is shown graphically in Figure A.1. (if you are using one of the other standards, simply ignore the non-applicable sections as shown in Figure 4 of the introduction to this book). There are five main groups of associated modules in the top part of the diagram. The bottom part includes five modules that affect all the other modules and it is suggested that you address these last. An attempt at writing the documentation for each group is tried before commencing on another. Each module must be addressed separately, but the grouping will also suggest that some information is common to the other module(s) in that group. Thus, for example, all the topics addressing inspection and testing are grouped with similar modules addressing test equipment for example.

If you consider how a contract is addressed and produced in your company and proceed in addressing the QA system in the same sequence, you will find that many of the requirements of the standards are in fact very easy to implement. When investigating each department within your company, consider it as a 'customer' of the previous department and a 'supplier' to the next department. For example, if we consider the design area as a supplier of information to the purchasing and production departments, we can very easily establish the specific requirements of these departments. Promoting this concept of each department being a customer constantly makes all employees aware of the company's customers and can beneficially introduce some competitiveness within your company.

The design and implementation of the system will not be a quick task and it is not suggested that you aim to get everything right in one module or group before addressing another area. Instead attempt each area (in document preparation and implementation) and have a path of continuous improvement reviewing each module systematically until it reaches the quality level of the standard. When designing the documentation adopt a hierarchical system, as shown in Figure A.2 by clearly separating and cross-referencing the different types of documents; policies – Part 1, methods – Part 2 and related forms – Appendices. This minimises the amount of editing required to the QA manual as changes are made.

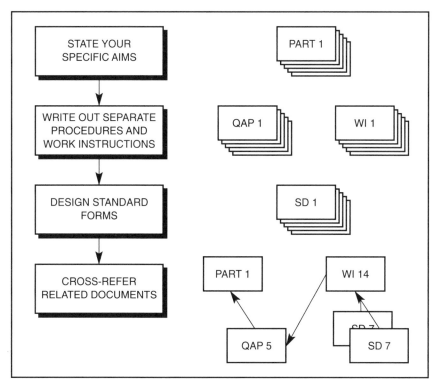

Figure A.2 Producing the QA manual

Figure A.3 shows the sequence of operation that is required in each cycle of reviewing the system. One contentious point deliberately raised is that of setting the levels of quality expected by each part of the system. All too often people make the mistake of attempting to introduce a system that is above the quality requirements of the customer. This may be admirable in its aim but can also use up valuable resources that could be invested elsewhere in the business. If we refer back to the comment in the preface to this book about the success of far Eastern companies, many products originating from there gained sales in Europe and America initially because of their reliability and not because they were 'new'. It was the resulting profits from these sales that later funded innovation and further success. Adopting a similar approach might prove just as beneficial to your company!

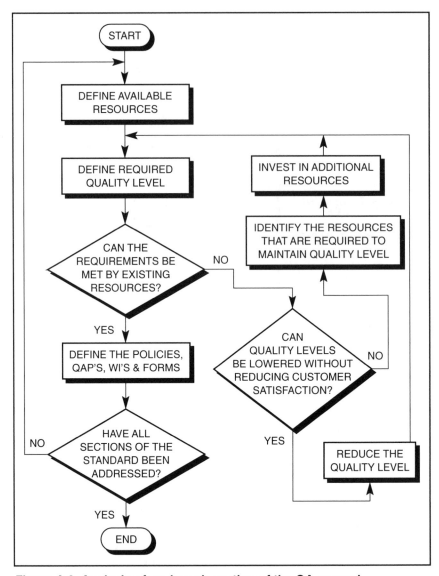

Figure A.3 Analysis of each each section of the QA manual

APPENDIX II

ISO 9000 and TQM – Total Quality Management

As we have seen, the ISO standards were derived from the needs of manufacturing industry and are product orientated. That is to say that, irrespective of the type of product, they concentrate on the different business functions that are required to produce a product and only address these areas. Procedures and methods are tightly controlled and the marketing, finance and indeed many other departments are completely ignored. The primary aim of an ISO9000 QA system is in fact to achieve 'technical' product reliability. Thus it is quite possible to consistently provide products that meet the customer's requirements but not market these effectively to keep the company in profit!

Total Quality Management differs in that its core aim is to address all business processes and aim to provide a complete quality service to the customer. This will include ensuring that the marketing and product development areas, for example, are actively involved in achieving a target level of quality set by the company. The Japanese are obvious masters of TQM as evidenced by their commitment to technical quality and their skills in product innovation and successful promotion of these products. In addition TQM lays much emphasis on giving employees the flexibility to quickly change their methods in order to adapt to the pressures of the open market.

Although ISO9000 systems and TQM are obviously approached differently, they are not exclusive to each other. If you are adopting the TQM approach, the ISO9000 system can be regarded as a sub-system of TQM. Since its aim is to provide technically reliable products, it can be readily broadened after introduction to involve the other business functions within your company. The additional TQM system manual can be treated as a separate item and excluded from the normal QA manual during ISO9000 auditing if necessary. As yet there is no international registration system comparable to that available for ISO9000 companies. Therefore, it is advisable to gain ISO9000 registration if at all possible as it is at least easily recognisable to potential customers and is a valuable marketing tool.

ISO9000/BS5750 – Exploding some myths

- ### Registered companies can only deal with other registered companies

There is no requirement for any registered company to deal with any particular company, registered or not. It is the complete responsibility of your company to manage the purchase of supplies and to ensure that these supplies are of suitable quality. However, it is well known that registered companies prefer to deal with other registered companies because it reduces management time and cost. For the same reasons, government bodies are tending to similarly prefer registered companies, when sourcing supplies.

- ### Paperwork drastically increases in the business

Very few companies actually see an increase in paperwork due to the introduction of ISO9000. However, many companies note that where previous 'informal' notes on contracts were acceptable, these must now be formalised and correctly filed. Thus the real consequence of using the QA system has been to formalise existing methods which have often been working very inefficiently. The 'blame' for an apparent increase in paperwork does not lie with the QA system but rather with the previous methods that were in operation.

- ### ISO9000 is only suitable for large companies

Company size based on turnover or number of employees is not addressed in the standards and companies of all sizes are successfully implementing ISO9000 QA systems worldwide. In small businesses one main problem is that personnel resources are usually limited and employees often carry out a range of tasks that would be separated in larger businesses. In addition, the costs of introduction can often drain the cash-flow and profits.

Both of these problems can be overcome by sharing the initial document and system preparation work across a range of staff and implementing the system over a longer period of time than is usual. In addition, some larger companies are willing to aid their regular suppliers in introducing systems by 'loaning' some of their resources such as their QA manager. The main cost of introduction usually is that of training staff and cost-sharing, by jointly hiring a consultant, with other small suppliers in a similar position is but one example of cost reduction. However remember, as stated in the introduction, that the consultant does not run the business and you should maintain a control on the introduction of the system.

• ISO9000 is not suitable for 'service' companies

As explained earlier, the standards originally evolved from the needs of manufacturing industry and the wording of the standards is orientated towards 'tangible' products such as cars rather than 'invisible' services such as those provided by an accountancy practice. Unlike manufacturing business where the supplied product is often mass-produced, service businesses concentrate on supplying products that are often greatly adapted to specific customer requirements. As an example an accountancy practice will usually take on client business only after investigating the special needs of the customer such as its regulatory audit requirements which might depend on company size or turnover.

However, all companies supply products; it is simply the form of the product that changes and the standards can be easily interpreted to service industries. As an example, Figure A.4 shows functions in an accountancy practice corresponding to ISO9001. This is not an 'official' interpretation but clearly demonstrates the flexibility of the standards and range of application in service in business. Many trade and professional organisations in the service areas are now producing interpretations of this standard to aid their members and you should contact the relative organisation if you are finding problems in implementing the standard.

ISO 9001 STANDARD – SECTIONS		INTERPRETATION FOR AN ACCOUNTANCY PRACTICE
TITLE	REF.	
Management Responsibility	4.1	Statement regarding the firm's commitment to quality
Quality System	4.2	The designed system defining its extent and use
Contract Review	4.3	Engagement/assignment conditions
Design Control	4.4	Design of particular service required by the client, including approximate times to complete work
Document Control	4.5	Maintaining the QA system and the client's records
Purchasing	4.6	Specification of services supplied by third-party consultants
Purchaser Supplied Product	4.7	Documents and data supplied by the client
Product Identification & Traceability	4.8	Identification of work completed and its source material (audit trails)
Process Control	4.9	Management of the client's work in accordance with the terms of engagement

Figure A.4 Application of ISO9001 to accountancy

ISO 9001 STANDARD – SECTIONS		INTERPRETATION FOR AN ACCOUNTANCY PRACTICE
TITLE	**REF.**	
Inspecting & Testing	4.10	Internal inspection of standard of work for clients
Inspection, measuring & test equipment	4.11	
Inspection & Test Status	4.12	Approval of work by senior staff after inspection
Control of non-conforming product	4.13	Redoing work where initial work did not meet the terms of engagement
Corrective Action	4.14	Review of complaints and errors in work
Handling, storage, packaging & delivery	4.15	Relates principally to safety and confidentiality of documents
Quality Records	4.16	Maintaining the records generated by the QA system
Internal Quality Audits	4.17	Review of the QA system and its effectiveness
Training	4.18	Adequate training of all staff
Servicing	4.19	Maintenance of service to long-term customers
Statistical Techniques	4.20	Used to decide on the frequency of internal audits and spot-checks on work

Figure A.4 Application of ISO9001 to accountancy (continued)

INDEX

Italics cross-refer to related documents in the sample QA manual

Further titles of interest

FINANCIAL TIMES

PITMAN PUBLISHING

ISBN	TITLE	AUTHOR
0 273 60561 5	Achieving Successful Product Change	Innes
0 273 03970 9	Advertising on Trial	Ring
0 273 60232 2	Analysing Your Competitor's Financial Strengths	Howell
0 273 60466 X	Be Your Own Management Consultant	Pinder
0 273 60168 7	Benchmarking for Competitive Advantage	Bendell
0 273 60529 1	Business Forecasting using Financial Models	Hogg
0 273 60456 2	Business Re-engineering in Financial Services	Drew
0 273 60069 9	Company Penalties	Howarth
0 273 60558 5	Complete Quality Manual	McGoldrick
0 273 03859 1	Control Your Overheads	Booth
0 273 60022 2	Creating Product Value	De Meyer
0 273 60300 0	Creating World Class Suppliers	Hines
0 273 60383 3	Delayering Organisations	Keuning
0 273 60171 7	Does Your Company Need Multimedia?	Chatterton
0 273 60003 6	Financial Engineering	Galitz
0 273 60065 6	Financial Management for Service Companies	Ward
0 273 60205 5	Financial Times Guide to Using the Financial Pages	Vaitilingam
0 273 60006 0	Financial Times on Management	Lorenz
0 273 03955 5	Green Business Opportunities	Koechlin
0 273 60385 X	Implementing the Learning Organisation	Thurbin
0 273 03848 6	Implementing Total Quality Management	Munro-Faure
0 273 60025 7	Innovative Management	Phillips
0 273 60327 2	Investor's Guide to Emerging Markets	Mobius
0 273 60622 0	Investor's Guide to Measuring Share Performance	Macfie
0 273 60528 3	Investor's Guide to Selecting Shares that Perform	Koch
0 273 60704 9	Investor's Guide to Traded Options	Ford
0 273 03751 X	Investor's Guide to Warrants	McHattie
0 273 03957 1	Key Management Ratios	Walsh
0 273 60384 1	Key Management Tools	Lambert
0 273 60259 4	Making Change Happen	Wilson
0 273 60424 4	Making Re-engineering Happen	Obeng
0 273 60533 X	Managing Talent	Sadler
0 273 60153 9	Perfectly Legal Competitor Intelligence	Bernhardt
0 273 60167 9	Profit from Strategic Marketing	Wolfe
0 273 60170 9	Proposals, Pitches and Beauty Parades	de Forte
0 273 60616 6	Quality Tool Kit	Mirams
0 273 60336 1	Realising Investment Value	Bygrave
0 273 60713 8	Rethinking the Company	Clarke
0 273 60328 0	Spider Principle	Linton
0 273 03873 7	Strategic Customer Alliances	Burnett
0 273 03949 0	Strategy Quest	Hill
0 273 60624 7	Top Intrapreneurs	Lombriser
0 273 03447 2	Total Customer Satisfaction	Horovitz
0 273 60201 2	Wake Up and Shake Up Your Company	Koch
0 273 60387 6	What Do High Performance Managers Really Do?	Hodgson

For further details or a full list of titles contact:

The Professional Marketing Department, Pitman Publishing, 128 Long Acre, London WC2E 9AN, UK

Tel +44 (0)71 379 7383 or fax +44 (0)71 240 5771